U.S. Corporate Investment in Taiwan

Jordan C. Schreiber   International Economics   Foreword by
Kenneth W. Sparks

U.S. Corporate Investment in Taiwan

The Dunellen Company, Inc., New York, New York

International Standard Book Number 0-8424-0002-8.

Library of Congress Catalogue Card Number 79-119338.

Printed in the United States of America.

Designed by Anspach Grossman Portugal, Inc.

To my wife, Martha, whose tolerance
during my preoccupation with this
research project enabled the work to
be completed; my son, Eric; and my
daughter, Nancy.

Foreword

The field of economic development has been the subject of an enormous volume of research and speculation in recent years. Techniques and principles from all disciplines have been introduced, to the point where no human activity, from reproduction to telecommunications, can be considered irrelevant. Since no one can claim to be more than casually familiar with subjects beyond his own area of experience and specialization, new and mutually irreconcilable theories of economic development are introduced, sometimes accepted, and in their turn swept away. Usually, a residue is left behind to bewilder further the interested observer. I do not believe the confusion could be any greater if all the participants deliberately had this result in mind.

Historically, when Western science has been confronted with such a bedlam of fact and speculation, the only way out has been to return to the study of the observable, related facts in a specific situation. This Dr. Schreiber's book does. It describes what actually happened in the case of Taiwan, and puts us into a world of manageable size, of comprehensible diversity, and of unquestionable economic development.

The particular feature of Taiwan's development that Dr. Schreiber finds of special interest is the role played by American private foreign investment. Fortunately, fairly reliable and complete statistics are available on the amounts and purposes of these investments, so their quantitative importance can be quite accurately assessed. What cannot be assessed is the impact of various incentives upon private investment decisions; how and what influenced the decision making, and the diverse, not-so-evident concerns of American businessmen in making overseas investments. Dr. Schreiber quite rightly considers these basic to stimulation of private foreign-investment inputs, without which economic growth would be limited or forced to pursue totalitarian paths. With the aid of private foreign capital, the transformation of the Taiwanese economy from traditional to modern forms has taken place in one of the shortest time spans known to economic historians.

Of course, as Dr. Schreiber points out, this transformation in Taiwan depended on much more than American investment and innovative stimulus. The period of Japanese control and, later, the U.S. aid program provided Taiwan with an economic and social infrastructure that would be the envy of all but a few less developed nations today. The final ingredients of immigration from the mainland and the incentive provided by the threat of the Chinese Communist regime were also important.

Given so many favorable conditions, there is perhaps a danger that the role of foreign investment may be somewhat overstressed, notwithstanding the author's attempts to present a balanced view of the inputs to Taiwan's development. Nonetheless, the argument that foreign investment does play the key role in normal economic development has a strong basis in the historical correlation between such investment and rapid economic growth in almost all the other examples we know of. The usual exceptions are Japan and the Soviet Union; but in these cases, only foreign equity ownership was omitted. All the other apparatus of foreign investment—industrial reorganization, imported managers and technicians, training of local personnel at the foreign suppliers' home factories, and so on—was present; the usually required foreign capital input was simply replaced with forced domestic savings. Aside from a few oil-rich nations, it is difficult to see how most of today's less developed countries could marshal the domestic resources or foreign exchange to imitate these examples, except through severe regimentation and suppression of consumption.

This latter alternative has been tried frequently and has succeeded occasionally, from pharaonic times through the present. It seems to depend, however, on a degree of internal political control that contemporary societies are unwilling to accept. (Cuba is the apparent exception; but then, it falls back into the category of Japan and the Soviet Union, which, when their economies were developing, imported all that foreign investment could provide, minus only investment in the very restricted sense of equity ownership. In the case of Cuba, even Soviet capital investment is there, to be repaid from long-term contracts for the supply of sugar.)

Thus, I think it can be fairly argued that the exceptions to the historical correlation between foreign investment and rapid economic growth are exceptions more in form than substance and that the remaining alternative of totalitarian control to yield forced savings is not acceptable to less developed countries today. So we return to Dr. Schreiber's example of Taiwan as a classical case of remarkable correlation between foreign investment and rapid economic growth. It follows the well-known sequences of modern times, beginning with the Dutch investment in the English woolen industry, through English investment in the United States and later the Argentine, right up to the contemporary examples of U.S. investment in Mexico, the backward regions of Belgium, and Taiwan itself.

In addition to examining economic development from a factual, or case-study, point of view, the value of which I pointed out in my opening comments, this book provides practical, topical information to those who are concerned with enhancing economic growth and/or capital investment in less developed countries of the world and to those in administrative governing positions in these countries who seek overseas capital and wish to create the conditions precedent to joining the ranks of the developed. For more than 300 years of modern history, private foreign investment has shown a remarkable ability to contribute to these conditions under a wide variety of environments. Taiwan is one of the most convincing examples, and being the most recent, is an unusually interesting and pertinent one.

Kenneth W. Sparks
Treasurer–ITT Africa and
the Middle East
International Telephone and
Telegraph Corporation

Preface

Foreign private capital, of which American corporations provide a major share, has been making a significant contribution to Taiwan by providing jobs, upgrading skills, helping to narrow the trade and payments gap, and introducing needed industries and technology.

With a view to the future, however, if the Republic of China is able to carry out its projected plan of economic development, possibly during the early 1980's, reliance upon foreign capital for economic sustenance will no longer be necessary. To meet this timetable, there will have to be political and social stability, as well as continued urbanization and family-planning programs. Therefore, although there should be a continuing desire to attract foreign capital for at least the next decade, this need for foreign capital is not interminable. The time may come when foreign capital may be viewed in a much less favorable light.

American corporations have a different frame of reference than does the Chinese government. Aside from the fundamental motivation to earn profits, American corporate management is intensely concerned with the degree of uncertainty and risk perceived in an investment situation, particularly in less-familiar overseas environments, where stability may be fragile. The AID (Agency for International Development) investment-guarantee program has assuaged but not eliminated this concern. Accordingly, with regard to foreign investments, corporate executives tend to take actions that reflect a short-range perspective and avoid the greater uncertainty inherent in longer-term commitments.

Although Taiwan is viewed, both currently and in the longer run, by American corporate investors as a low-risk situation, and assured markets and tax concessions make profits more certain, an almost instinctive desire to protect and to hasten the return of invested capital persists. Various devices are used by almost all American corporations in Taiwan in order to reduce risk.

The United States government is faced with a potential conflict situation. Currently the political benefit of private American investment in developing nations overshadows the adverse effect upon the balance of payments. The investment guarantee program helps to encourage such investment. In the longer term, however, the investment guarantee program may bind the United States to a position in favor of a status quo which may not be in the nation's best political interest.

The Chinese incentive program, in general, has been reasonable, from the point of view of both the host country and the foreign corporations, being neither overly generous nor competitively inadequate compared with the incentive programs of other developing nations. One item, the low corporate maximum tax rate, is singled out as perhaps representing an unnecessary concession. It is questioned whether future attitudes of Chinese governmental leaders toward foreign capital, if development programs are successfully implemented, will remain as favorable as at present. Although, currently, the goals of American corporations and the Chinese Government coincide in the form of industrial activity, many events, including successful development, might lead to a divergence of interest in the future.

What policies and programs should American corporations take in Taiwan with a view toward these possible future developments? Might not a step to moderate future tensions be the sale to the Taiwan public of equity in the American-established enterprise? Further study in this prospective problem area is suggested.

Acknowledgments

This book owes its existence to the remarkable spirit of cooperativeness and disclosure which generally prevails among publicly owned American corporations today. A large majority of the companies with operations or projected activity in Taiwan who were contacted, and from whom specific information was requested regarding aspects of their Taiwan projects, were most accommodating. Because of a desire on the part of several of the corporate officials to remain anonymous, neither companies nor management interviewees and respondents may be named in this book, but I wish to express a feeling of gratitude for their collective cooperation.

I wish also to express my thanks to officials of the China Industrial Trade Office in New York, various officers of the U.S. State and Commerce Departments, and most important, Professors Kyung-won Kim and Paul Alpert of the New York University Graduate School of Arts and Science, for their guidance and counsel; to Paule H. Jones of the Dunellen Company, for her expert editorial advice; and to Eugene H. Nellen, President of that organization. Finally I wish to acknowledge my complete responsibility for the study and its conclusions.

Contents

List of Tables

Abbreviations

AID   Agency for International Development

CIDC   Chinese Industrial and Development Center

CITO   Chinese Investment and Trade Office

CUSA   Taiwan Joint Committee on United States Aid

ECA   Economic Cooperation Administration

ECAFE United Nations Economic Commission for Asia and the Far East

GRC   Government of the Republic of China

KEPZ   Kaohsiung Export Processing Zone

UNRRA United Nations Relief and Rehabilitation Administration

U.S. Corporate Investment in Taiwan

1   **Introduction**

Since the early 1960's, the relatively small island of Taiwan, now the seat of the Republic of China, has become a rapidly developing economic entity. Through the combination of an energetic and intelligent population, massive United States aid, and a legacy, from Japanese rule, of organization, education, and acceptance of technology, Taiwan has become one of the few developing nations to "graduate" from the American aid program. This has been done despite a paucity of natural resources and a government that wore a mantle of failure for its management of the mainland China economy.

The economic thrust since 1951 has been one of emphasis on the private sector of the economy. This stress upon the private sector since cessation of economic aid from the United States in 1965 has extended to virtual dependence upon private foreign capital as the means to help sustain growth. And with one of the highest population growth rates in the world and an almost continuous pattern of trade deficits, continued economic growth is essential to Taiwan.

American corporations have been and are expected to continue to be a most important source of capital, with Japanese corporations and overseas Chinese comprising almost all of the balance of foreign investment.

In the face of a drastically increased balance-of-payments deficit following the British devaluation of the pound, President Johnson ordered mandatory limits to corporate direct overseas investments, starting in 1968.[1] This came at a time when there is increasing concern in the world over the impact of a "third force," United States overseas corporate investment. The sheer magnitude of private American investment is awesome.

The apprehensions of many world political leaders are aroused. Reasons for anxiety about the effect of United States private capital are political, economic, and social in nature and include nationalism, ideological antipathy to capitalism, and resistance to change. Specific concerns include the possible discouragement of domestic research and development and widening of the American technological lead and the difficulties that might ensue when U.S. subsidiaries overseas are subject both to the laws of the United States and to those of the country in which it is doing business.

For example, with regard to the latter point, might not a conflict arise when American subsidiaries overseas have opportunities, permissible under U.S. law, to trade profitably with other countries but are forbidden to do so by host-country policy?

While there are anxieties and questions as to the role of American capital in some parts of the world, it is in great demand in other areas. This congeries of anxiety, interest, and controversy raises a key question: What are the motivations and modus operandi of private American companies overseas?

This study will reduce the question to microcosmic proportion and describe the attitudes and actions, and the implications thereof, of United States corporations in one country—the Republic of China on Taiwan.

The Republic of China is a country that vigorously seeks American capital investment, despite seemingly contrary attitudes in the past. As of September, 1967, $121.5 million has been invested or approved for investment by 91 American companies in Taiwan.[2] Taiwan is therefore an area where aspects and implications of the inflow of American capital may be observed.

To what extent do the motivations and expectations of the American corporate investors coincide with the current and future aims of the Government of the Republic of China? In a broad sense, that question is the core of this study. More specifically, what are the motivations and expectations of American investment in Taiwan?

A descriptive framework of the more poignant aspects focuses upon

(a) the reasons for and the nature of American corporate investment;

(b) the corporate perspective *vis-à-vis* other investment opportunities;

(c) the assessed risk and the protective devices used to safeguard investment;

(d) the possible implications, as well as the present meaningfulness, of United States governmental activities related to private investment;

(e) the importance and relevance of incentives for attraction of corporate capital.

This is an empirical study intended to describe and explain actual corporate behavior. At least two other empirical studies of American private corporate investment behavior have been undertaken. In one, Yair Aharoni describes aspects of American corporate investment in Israel, with stress upon the decision-making process.[3] The other work, edited by Raymond F. Mikesell, is an analysis of an extensive survey of direct American corporate investment overseas.[4]

These two works had an underlying hypothesis which in essence said, "Here is how and why investment decisions were really made. The actual foreign investment decision process bears little resemblance to the explanation offered by theoretical economics." The authors then proceed to describe and to explain seemingly irrational behavior patterns.

A phenomenon described by Aharoni and Mikesell and also found by this writer is the great diversity of reasons for and aspects of foreign investment. To a great extent, many conventional ideas regarding corporate operations are put into question by the sheer number of approaches to a problem.

An attempt will be made here not only to explain actual corporate reactions—which may derive from unreal preconceptions—but to relate them to governmental policies and programs. Data and information are based on field research consisting of extensive semistructured interviews and a mail questionnaire survey of appropriate executives of 30 American companies with business interests in Taiwan.

The sample constitutes a sizable proportion (approximately one third) of American companies with investments in Taiwan. Moreover, the sample is representative, in terms of company size and nature of industry, of all American corporations with activity there. (A description of the interview and questionnaire mailing technique, including facsimiles of relevant letters and lists of questions, is to be found in the Appendix.)

Overall, the cooperativeness, and willingness to disclose information quite basic to corporate operations in competitive fields, was noteworthy. Of the 24 companies from whom interviews were requested, 20 granted them. Sometimes staff specialists, as well as the line manager, were available to answer questions. Often relevant files were opened to inspection.

The mailing also elicited good response. Rather extensive questionnaires were completed and returned by 10 of the 24 companies to whom they were sent.

The nature of some of the information supplied is confidential, and therefore the names of companies have not been revealed nor have case studies been made.

Notes

1. "Restrictions announced on American private overseas investments," *Wall Street Journal,* January 2, 1968, p. 3.

2. M. C. Liu, "Investment Opportunities in Taiwan," statements made at seminar on Industrial Opportunities in Taiwan, sponsored by Chinese Institute of Engineers, New York, November 4, 1967.

3. Yair Aharoni, *The Foreign Investment Decision Process* (Boston: Harvard University, Graduate School of Business Administration, Division of Research, 1966).

4. Raymond F. Mikesell, ed., *United States Private and Government Investment Abroad* (Eugene, Oregon: University of Oregon, 1962).

2   The Relationship Between the United States and Taiwan

Taiwan, as the island of Formosa has always been called in the Orient, was populated successively by disparate groups of ethnic Chinese having different linguistic, socioeconomic, and cultural features. Until 1895 the island was administered quite loosely by Chinese dynastic authority, despite incursions by the Portuguese, Dutch, Spanish, and French, in that order, after the beginning of the 17th century. In that year, the treaty of Shimonoseki formally ended the Sino-Japanese War of 1894-1895 and provided for the cession of Taiwan by China, and the island became the first colony of rapidly modernizing Japan.

While Japan basically followed a course of exploitation in Taiwan, it also created an infrastructure consisting of an efficient agricultural base, roads, communications, port facilities, and most important, a literate population receptive to technological advance and change. This legacy survived the turmoil and destruction of World War II and the immediate postwar years, when the Chinese Nationalists seemingly regarded the island as an occupied enemy territory.

Economic Aid

Shortly after the cessation of World War II, Taiwan began to receive aid from the United Nations Relief and Rehabilitation Administration (UNRRA), which got the bulk of its funds from the United States. In early 1949, the United States initiated direct economic aid to Taiwan, under provisions of the China Aid Act of 1948. The sum of $338 million (reduced to $275 million under later legislation) was authorized for one year, to be provided and administered by the Economic Cooperation Administration (ECA).

Economic aid was intended to remove a major cause of war and the political chaos upon which the Communists thrive: economic instability. The China Aid Act declared it to be "the policy of the people of the United States to encourage the Republic of China and its people to exert sustained common efforts which will speedily achieve the internal peace and economic stability in China which are essential for lasting peace and prosperity in the world."[1] The China Aid Act, in addition to providing economic aid, established the Joint Commission on Rural Reconstruction (JCRR) in China to "carry out a program for reconstruction in rural areas of China."[2]

In March 1949, as the military and economic position of the Nationalists was collapsing, the Department of State supported an ECA proposal to extend use of uncommitted but appropriated funds until the end of 1949 in those areas of China not under Communist control. Congress passed legislation which embodied this proposal and, in fact, extended the fund availability date until February 15, 1950.[3]

ECA operations on Taiwan had actually begun in January 1949. A private New York technical consulting firm, J. G. White Engineering Corporation, was engaged, in the absence of sufficient technical expertise among Chinese governmental or United States Mission representatives, to give advice on industrial projects. An advisory committee of Chinese and Americans, representing concerned departments and organizations, was organized to help in economic planning and to coordinate Chinese self-help efforts with ECA aid. This was the Taiwan Joint Committee on United States Aid (CUSA).[4]

In the face of military and political uncertainty, United States economic assistance to Taiwan in 1950 consisted of meeting short-range urgent needs by supplying critically short commodities and petroleum, so as to provide relief, ease inflation, and permit the repair of essential industrial machinery.[5] Only $48 million was used to finance the ECA activity in Taiwan during 1950.[6] It was obviously a quite limited aid effort, with a limited goal—to effect some alleviation of economic distress so that military forces would not have to be diverted from defense of Taiwan against a possible Communist assault.

After the Korean hostilities started, substantial United States economic, as well as military, aid became earmarked for Taiwan. The actual arrival of aid material allocated after the Korean outbreak (and reflecting a reversal of American policy) started in 1951.

The $48 million obligation for economic assistance in 1950 was committed as follows:[7]

Commodity Program	$32,982,000
Industrial Maintenance and Replacement Program	11,716,000
Ocean Freight	2,758,000
Technical Assistance	443,000
Joint Commission on Rural Reconstruction	194,000
Other Expenditures	60,000
Total	$48,153,000

One fourth ($8.2 million) of the funds spent for commodities went toward the purchase of chemical fertilizer to revitalize rice growing. Imports of raw cotton ($6.0 million), soybeans ($4.7 million), flour ($2.5 million), peanuts ($1.8 million), crude oil ($1.7 million), lumber ($1.4 million), and peanut oil ($1.2 million) followed in importance.[8] The major industrial maintenance and replacement program outlays were to utilities such as power and communications and transportation systems. It may be seen that the entire program had military relevance.

As the United States Seventh Fleet position in the Taiwan Strait reduced military pressures, aid focus turned toward the critical economic and financial position in which the Nationalist Government on Taiwan found itself. Early in 1951, and on an annual basis thereafter until 1965, allocations of funds were made for economic assistance to Taiwan. With the easing of inflationary pressures, the basic needs of the population were met, and programs and projects were instituted which had as their aim the increase of Chinese ability for self-support. In a step to further this purpose, the United States contributed toward the first Republic of China Four Year Development Plan (1953-56).

In the middle and late 1950's, aid funds were increasingly given to infrastructure and industrial projects. As economic progress was made and plan growth-rate goals were continually exceeded, another shift in U.S. assistance goals for Taiwan took form: "There was a gradual reduction in emphasis upon general economic development and an increasing emphasis upon the aims of fostering private enterprise, promoting exports, and terminating U.S. concessional assistance."[9]

United States aid was terminated in mid-1965, but the emphasis placed upon private enterprise in the later stages of the assistance program not only eased the phase-out and discontinuance of external aid but provided the impetus for continued economic growth. United States economic assistance to Taiwan, if we dismiss the relatively minor efforts in 1949 and 1950, spanned fifteen years, from 1951 through 1965, and involved a total of $1.5 billion. Obligated and actual disbursements of aid funds, as opposed to obligations incurred, extended to 1968, and reflected the long lead-time in getting delivery of certain items. Overall, American economic aid obligations averaged about $100 million a year during the 1951-65 period, contrasted with roughly $165 million a year for military aid furnished during the same period.[10] American aid to Taiwan was substantial relative to Taiwan's economy. Over the 1952-63 period, economic aid (including loans and capital, which were negligible overall) averaged about 34 percent of Taiwan's total gross investment.[11] As the economy grew, the proportionate importance of U.S. aid decreased.

How were the assistance funds allocated by sector of the economy?

> More than two-thirds of all U.S. capital assistance—aid-generated local currency as well as U.S. dollars—went to infrastructure and agriculture .... Aid financed nearly three-quarters of all net investments made in Taiwan's infrastructure during 1951-63, well over half of that made in agriculture, but only about one-eighth of that made in industry.[12]

Four fifths of U.S. aid went to the public sector, and less than one fifth to private enterprises.[13] As economic development progressed, the preponderance of private investment went into the industrial sector. Thus, the pattern of heavy allocation of U.S. assistance to infrastructure complemented the private sector and provided a base which generated growth. And the private sector did grow impressively, with a 1967 level that was over 12 times that of 1952 and a rise in its share of total industrial production from 42.7 percent to 70.3 percent for the same period.[14]

Aid to infrastructure included allocations to expand electrical power generation and distribution to build highways, bridges, and railways, to develop harbors, and to provide telegraph and telephone facilities.[15]

The agricultural aid was channeled through the JCRR and consisted largely of technical assistance and training, land and water-resource development, crop and livestock development, land reform, and rural health, forestry, and fisheries programs.

Other major aid activity included the construction of school buildings and aid to industry through "grants and loans to private and public enterprises, initially for their rehabilitation and modernization and later for their initiation or expansion."[16] The grants and loans were made either directly or through financial intermediaries such as the China Development Corporation. In the later stage of the aid program, there was "technical assistance to the Chinese government on measures to improve the climate for private investment." These measures presaged the termination of aid and included the institution of laws, regulations, and incentives to encourage private investment. (These will be discussed in detail in Chapter 2).

AID also sought to induce the Chinese government to transfer the public industrial enterprises to private hands. Although the national and provincial governments voiced agreement, action has not been taken, probably because of reluctance to add to the unemployment problem by the inevitable whittling down of customarily overstaffed public agencies if denationalization took place.

The composition of United States economic assistance funds for Taiwan was as follows:[17]

AID Assistance
    Grants $ 949.9 million
    Loans   159.8 million
                      Total $1,109.7 million

Public Law 480
    Grants $ 373.2 million
    Loans   62.7 million
                      Total $ 435.9 million

Of the total aid given to Taiwan over the 15-year period 1951-65, almost two thirds ($915 million) was related to maintenance of the armed forces, which is considered economic aid rather than part of the Military Assistance Program. These funds were used to replace funds directed from the economy to keep military strength at a certain level. This included financing the import of commodities on a continuing basis, military construction, and provisions and material directly consumed by the armed forces.

Public Law 480, which accounted for one quarter of the economic assistance, provides for surplus agricultural commodities to be sold abroad for U.S. dollars or for local currency or to be given away outright. Of the aid supplied to Taiwan under Public Law 480, 58 percent was in the form of sales for local currency (Title I), 9 percent consisted of grants (Title II), 19 percent was grants to voluntary relief agencies who administered distribution to those in need (Title III), and 14 percent was sales requiring payment in U.S. dollars (Title IV).[18]

With this combination of statutory sources of funds, most aid projects were financed by a mix of "U.S. dollars, aid-generated NT dollars, and funds supplied by the Chinese sponsor from local resources."[19]

It is apparent that United States aid energized private investment by playing a major role in building infrastructure, using local currency for developmental purposes, and defraying military support costs which would otherwise have diverted from capital formation.

The cooperative spirit and dedication of Chinese and American participants in the aid program has been noted by observers[20] and is in marked contrast to the situation that had existed on the mainland. There is evidence of recognition by the Chinese Nationalists of their shortsightedness in effecting reform and hope that they will regain the respect of the mainland Chinese people by the contrast of their economic achievements with that of the Communists.[21]

United States aid played a monumental role in Taiwan's economic development. The very success of this development—in 1965, Taiwan was second, in Asia, after Japan, in per capita income; had one of the highest rates of increase of gross national product and industrial production in the world; and was a leading agricultural producer in terms of efficiency—led to the discontinuance of United States aid.

The Taiwan experience has been unique in the magnitude of progress that has been made and the country is a showcase in the developing world. The amount of economic aid in 1951-65 ($1.5 billion) was large relative to that received by other developing nations in Asia and it helped the Republic of China to achieve self-sustaining economic growth; and as the economy grew, aid became decreasingly significant. The data in Table 1 indicate the dimensions of these achievements.

Notwithstanding these successes, Taiwan's economy suffers from imbalances, for the most part due to one of the highest population growth rates and population densities in the world. The resultant problems are high unemployment; chronic excess of imports over exports; shrinking farm size; and a "brain drain," partly due to low academic and research salaries. Underlying this latter problem is the need to expand infrastructure in the form of human and public resources so that a growing and self-sustaining economy may be adequately served.

Solutions to these problems require capital, which in capital-starved Taiwan, with the cessation of American economic

Table 1

Magnitude and Pattern of Foreign Aid to ECAFE Region Developing Countries

	1956/57–1963/64 Compound annual rate of GNP growth at constant prices	Net assistance: per cent of GNP at current prices		Change in % of GNP	Population in millions		Income per head, constant prices in U.S. dollars		Net assistance per head, in U.S. dollars	
		1956/57	1963/64		1956	1964	1956/57	1963/64	1956/57	1963/64
Burma	4.5	3.49	1.73	-1.76	20.79	24.23	57.63	68.77	2.12	1.20
Ceylon	3.6	0.79	1.89	1.10	8.93	10.96	119.94	128.84	1.00	2.62
China (Taiwan)	7.6	7.80	2.01	-5.79	9.24	12.07	117.70	154.32	10.26	4.01
India	4.1	1.30	2.81	1.51	394.22	471.62	65.07	73.56	0.78	2.32
Korea, Republic of	5.8	10.75	7.28	-3.47	22.04	27.63	111.63	135.82	16.31	8.33
Pakistan	4.4	2.89	5.44	2.55	85.26	100.76	67.59	78.01	1.94	3.76
Philippines	4.5	0.98	0.68	-0.30	24.29	31.27	191.20	208.88	1.93	1.14
Thailand	6.6	2.05	2.50	0.45	23.45	29.70	80.49	102.15	1.79	2.94

Source: United Nations, *Economic Survey of Asia and the Far East, 1966* (Bangkok, 1967), Tables I-2-2, I-2-3.

aid, can come from two sources: foreign loans and private foreign investment.

Post-Aid Involvement of the United States

In terminating the program of economic assistance, the United States has taken steps which have had a bearing upon continued Taiwanese economic development.

As noted, the financial terms of United States aid were diverse and ranged in nature from outright grants to soft loans repayable in local or in U.S. currency to "hard" loans (over 3½ percent interest).[22] As Taiwan's economic position improved, the aid terms veered toward those of the hard loans. Taiwan's successful record in meeting debt obligations on these hard loans put her in good position to secure loans from the world's financial institutions.

Indeed, Taiwan had already secured loans from nongovernmental U.S. institutions prior to aid termination and had established a domestic institution to channel and coordinate the use of loan funds. This was the China Development Corporation, which was a quasi-public organization established to lend funds to or invest in local private business. A $10 million loan from the Development Loan Fund was a major source of initial capital in 1959. In 1962 the China Development Corporation secured a loan from the International Development Association, and in 1964 a loan from the World Bank.[23]

The Republic of China had established a sound credit rating by the time United States economic aid ceased, a rating that has facilitated the obtaining of additional loans from such sources as the World Bank and the United States Export-Import Bank. Direct military aid in the form of military advisory groups and armaments has continued. To the extent that Chinese Communist forces are tied down in Fukien Province to prevent a possible Nationalist landing, these forces are not available for aggressive action elsewhere. Viewed in this light, military aid to the Republic of China is of direct strategic benefit to the United States.

The Vietnam War led to United States procurement of iron and steel manufactures, cement, textiles, and chemicals from Taiwan. Moreover, spending by United States servicemen on leave from

Vietnam reached an estimated rate of $1,000,000 per year by mid-1967, as 5,000 per month took rest and recreation leave in Taiwan. The availability of hotel facilities, a component of the development planning, was a factor in attracting the men and many of their dependents.[24]

The economic assistance program, of course, maintained American exports to Taiwan at a high level, as a large proportion of goods and services had to be procured in the United States. Currently, the chief Taiwan imports from the United States are raw cotton, wheat, soybeans, iron and steel scrap, machinery and tools, internal combustion engines, and tobacco. The decline of the U.S. share of Taiwan's imports is indicated in Table 2.

As a reflection of the falloff in U.S. aid-financed imports as the reason for decline in the U.S. share of total imports, the percentage of nonaid imports from the United States increased from 20 percent in 1962 to 26 percent in 1966.[25] Intense Japanese competition has also contributed to the decline of the United States share.

United States governmental efforts to increase exports to Taiwan include commercial and industrial exhibitions, organized by the Department of Commerce, after a research study shows a market for the product category. The first such activity of this sort was a United States Industrial Machinery Exhibition in Taipei in October and November 1967.[26]

The Department of Commerce also aids American exporters by providing appropriate market, legal, and economic data, and in March 1965 the department sent a United States trade and investment mission, composed of businessmen, to Taiwan to promote sale of American goods and services. The extension of credit as a device to stimulate trade was undertaken in 1967, when the United States Export-Import Bank approved a $5 million credit to finance Taiwan imports of American machinery and equipment. While the United States has been selling less in Taiwan, it has been buying more in recent years. Nevertheless, despite this trend the United States continues to have a decidedly favorable balance of trade with Taiwan. Major Taiwan exports to the United States are plywood, clothing, sugar, canned mushrooms, canned pineapples, and plastic manufactures. The export pattern is shown in Table 3.

Table 2

Pattern of Imports by Countries of Origin
(in percentages)

Year	United States	Japan	Germany	Philippines	Others
1953	51.2	28.5	0.8	0.1	19.4
1954	52.4	30.3	0.9	0.3	16.1
1955	47.0	30.9	3.2	0.3	18.6
1956	37.0	34.7	2.9	0.8	24.6
1957	37.0	33.6	3.3	0.5	25.6
1958	37.3	35.1	2.5	0.7	24.4
1959	33.5	39.4	5.9	1.5	19.7
1960	40.8	34.6	4.5	1.0	19.1
1961	43.2	32.1	3.7	1.5	19.5
1962	43.3	32.7	3.7	2.1	18.2
1963	44.8	28.8	3.2	3.1	20.1
1964	34.1	34.2	3.5	2.5	25.7
1965	34.4	37.0	3.9	2.5	22.2
1966	32.1	38.0	4.2	2.4	23.3
1967	31.9	37.2	3.4	1.8	25.7

Source: *Taiwan Statistical Data Book: 1968*, Table 10-12.

Table 3

Pattern of Exports by Countries of Destination
(in percentages)

Year	United States	Japan	Vietnam-Cambodia-Laos	Germany	Hong Kong	Others
1953	5.5	46.4	---	0.6	9.6	37.9
1954	4.8	53.9	0.1	1.7	8.8	31.7
1955	4.3	60.6	1.2	0.9	5.0	28.0
1956	4.8	35.5	2.1	1.8	7.2	48.6
1957	2.6	38.9	3.5	1.2	9.2	44.6
1958	6.1	43.9	2.4	3.2	5.5	38.9
1959	9.3	42.7	2.9	2.6	9.8	32.7
1960	12.5	37.4	2.0	2.3	11.5	34.3
1961	21.2	28.4	5.7	2.8	11.6	30.3
1962	24.6	24.3	9.3	4.7	9.9	27.2
1963	16.3	33.1	9.4	4.0	8.0	29.2
1964	18.1	30.2	8.4	3.9	7.2	32.2
1965	20.0	31.1	9.2	6.5	5.8	27.4
1966	19.7	24.9	15.8	5.5	5.9	28.2
1967	22.7	19.5	11.5	6.2	7.4	32.7

Source: *Taiwan Statistical Data Book: 1968,* Table 10-11.

American purchases from Taiwan in 1967 were $148 million, a 32 percent increase from $112 million in 1965.[27] The United States and Japan are the dominant trading partners of Taiwan.

U.S. Political Pressure Groups

Certain aspects of Taiwan's development have not been welcomed by all groups in the United States. Two stand out in this regard. One is the domestic mushroom industry (centered in the region of Lancaster, Pennsylvania), which is concerned over lower-priced competition from Taiwan. Another is the book publishing trade, which has been affected by the thriving "book-piracy" in Taiwan. English-language books are reproduced and sold to English-speaking tourists, businessmen, and United States servicemen on leave in Taiwan without payment of royalties or permission of copyright owners. As the Republic of China does not recognize international copyright agreements, the practice is legal in Taiwan. There is concern about the smuggling of books to places where English is read widely.[28] It is likely that other American interests (i.e., the textile-manufacturing, pineapple, and asparagus industries) are concerned about Taiwanese competition.

On the other hand, various American groups are developing an increased vested interest in preserving unrestricted trade with Taiwan for their products. The China Lobby, in addition to upholding the political integrity of the Republic of China vis-à-vis Communist China, is by and large also interested in strengthening economic ties and represents a pressure group toward this end.

U.S. Government Attitude Toward Private Investment

The balance-of-payments deficit has prompted the United States government to pursue policies to help increase exports. The sudden and drastically worsened balance-of-payments deficit in late 1967, which followed the British devaluation, led to a Presidential administrative action to impose mandatory limits upon direct overseas investment.

U.S. investment restrictions vary, falling into three categories—those affecting Western Europe; those affecting less developed countries, including Taiwan; and special exceptions (Canada, Japan, Australia, Great Britain, and oil-producing nations).

The most lenient restriction is placed upon investment in less developed countries, which is limited to 110% of a company's average annual investment in these countries in the base period 1965-66.

The greatest impact of the restrictions falls on Western Europe, where the preponderance of U.S. private investment is centered. The U.S. government therefore continues to favor private investment that contributes to economic development.

In addition to the investment surveys and the investment information promulgated by the Department of Commerce, there is the AID program of investment guarantees.

The AID Investment-Guarantee Program

U.S. investors in selected developing countries, including the Republic of China, may apply to AID for protection of their investment (including future retained earnings) against (1) inconvertibility; (2) expropriation; and (3) war, revolution, or insurrection.[29] There is no limit on the size of the investment to be insured, but it must first be approved by the host country and then by AID. The maximum protection for equity investments is 200 percent of the value of the investment, of which 100 percent covers future retained earnings; for loan investments, the sum of principal and interest; and for licensing and technical assistance agreements, the sum of the royalties or fees that can reasonably be expected over the life of the license or agreement.

To further governmental goals with regard to reduction of the balance-of-payments deficit, the investment must result in substantial procurement of U.S. goods.

The contract is for 20 years, and annual fees are ¼ of 1 percent of the coverage amount for convertibility and ½ of 1 percent each (7/8 of 1 percent if combined) for expropriation and for war.

As AID has not yet had to settle a claim, questions that might arise, such as what constitutes a war or insurrection, have not been clarified.

The effect of the AID investment-guarantee program is to remove consideration of such factors as uncontrollable, uncertain, and often unknown political and sociocultural conditions from the overseas investment decision.

U.S. Income Tax Regulations

Until 1962, with very few exceptions, taxes levied upon U.S. corporate income derived from overseas operations were the same as those levied on domestic income. A tax credit was given for foreign taxes paid. (An exception to this general rule was income earned in non-Communist-held areas of China, which in accordance with the China Trade Act of 1922 incurred a lower effective tax rate and which will be discussed shortly.)

While the eventual tax treatment was the same, certain loopholes were available to overseas income. Tax avoidance or deferral was possible for foreign subsidiaries (but not U.S. foreign branches), as tax was imposed on foreign-source income only when the income was actually returned to the United States in the form of dividends. This had the effect of (1) increasing the attractiveness of foreign, as opposed to domestic, investment; (2) causing an outflow of capital, thereby weakening the U.S. balance of payments; and (3) reducing U.S. tax revenue by encouraging delay in repatriation of earnings.[30]

Another problem peculiar to foreign-source income was that tax havens (countries with little or no tax on foreign-source income) might be used as a base for foreign operations in a third country. Tax havens included such micro-states as Liechtenstein, Monaco, and San Marino.

To defer payment of United States taxes and as a way to generate capital more rapidly for new investment or reinvestment, income funds could be accumulated overseas. When it is kept in mind that the federal tax structure is a means not only to derive revenue but also to encourage social and economic change, certain other aspects of the treatment of foreign-source income must be cited. When the United States was seeking to rehabilitate Western Europe in the immediate post-World War II period, American private capital was a welcome supplement to this public effort.

By the late 1950's, however, as Western Europe and Japan were "on their feet," and, indeed, were becoming formidable competitors as well as attractive markets for the United States, public policy changed. The balance of payments deficit starting in

1958 prompted concern over the flow of dollars overseas. Capital that was invested overseas but not repatriated within a reasonable time in the form of dividends represented a drain that adversely affected the balance of payments. The tax haven device was a clear abuse that posed possible adverse political, as well as economic, problems to the United States.

In the early 1960's, as the Kennedy administration took office, there was concern over the low rate of economic growth in the United States. It was recognized that dollars earned overseas had advantages over those earned domestically, because taxes could be deferred and funds were accordingly diverted that might have helped to stimulate the domestic economy. Despite these considerations that weigh against the investment of private capital overseas, the public policy of the United States, as exemplified by the foreign aid program, was to help underdeveloped nations to modernize their economies in order to provide for their burgeoning and politically awakened populations.

To reflect public policy, taxation of foreign-source income faced the need to correct abuses and encourage repatriation of earnings but, at the same time, provide incentive to continued capital flow to developing nations. Measures to meet these needs were incorporated in the Revenue Act of 1962. The deferral of the U.S. tax on certain categories of income made by "controlled foreign corporations" was ended. A "controlled foreign corporation" was defined as a foreign corporation with more than 50 percent of its voting power and value owned by U.S. shareholders. Each U.S. shareholder possessing a 10 percent or more interest in an American-controlled foreign corporation was required to include in gross income his pro rata share of the foreign corporation's "foreign base-company income," which is the income reduced to reflect "deductions (including taxes) properly allocable to such income."[31]

The effect of the new law was to levy U.S. corporate income tax upon foreign-source income, whether or not repatriated, not only upon directly owned foreign branches of American companies, as heretofore, but also upon American-controlled but foreign-incorporated subsidiaries.

Provisions were also made to discourage "third-country tax havens" and "unreasonable accumulation of earnings," to stimulate exports and thereby help the balance of payments.[32]

To encourage private investment in less developed countries, "dividends, interest, and net gains may be excluded from foreign base company income if derived from qualified investments in less developed countries," provided that equivalent funds are invested to replace those repatriated. The countries that would be considered "less developed" were indicated, and included Taiwan.[33]

Bilateral treaties were entered into by the United States and a number of other nations, including the Republic of China, to clarify and agree upon which of the two governments had taxable power over which segments of foreign-derived income. The attempt was to avoid double taxation of the same income.

The China Trade Act

The China Trade Act was enacted in 1922 to stimulate American business activity in the China area. It is one of the earliest examples of foreign policy affecting the United States tax structure.[34]

The criteria for constitution of China Trade Act companies are that "the Secretary of Commerce must find that they are organized to do business within 'China' [restricted since 1950 to Hong Kong and Taiwan], and that they will aid in developing markets in China for goods produced in the United States." Importation into Hong Kong and Taiwan of American capital equipment and raw materials incident to establishment of a manufacturing operation is deemed to comply with the intent of the law and will provide eligibility under the China Trade Act.[35]

The tax relief granted to China Trade Act companies takes the form of an exemption from the companies' taxable income of the earnings from business within Taiwan and Hong Kong. The consequent tax savings cannot exceed the amount of the distribution to stockholders of a special dividend.[36] In addition, individual stockholders of China Trade Act companies who reside in Hong Kong or Taiwan are exempted from federal income tax on dividends received.[37]

Summary

We have seen how United States economic aid to Taiwan contributed toward building the infrastructure and agricultural sector of the Taiwan economy and at the same time energized the private sector. As the aid program came to a close, the continuing need, in order to reduce unemployment and sustain economic growth, was for capital from private sources. Notwithstanding a balance-of-payments deficit, the United States government, through promotional activity, the guarantee of investment, and favorable income tax procedures, furthered the public policy of encouragement of private American investment in less developed countries, including Taiwan.

What actions did the government of the Republic of China take to encourage an inflow of private capital? The next chapter discusses this and how and why American corporations undertook business ventures in Taiwan.

Notes

1. U.S., Department of State, Division of Publications, Office of Public Affairs, *United States Relations with China with Special Reference to the Period 1944-1949*, Publication 3573, Far Eastern Series 30 (Washington, D.C.: Government Printing Office, 1949), p. 992.

2. Ibid.

3. Ibid., pp. 408-409.

4. Joseph Ballantine, *Formosa* (Washington, D.C.: The Brookings Institution, 1952), p. 134.

5. U.S., Economic Cooperation Administration, Mission to China, *U.S. Economic Assistance to Formosa, January 1 to December 31, 1950* (Washington, D.C.: Government Printing Office, 1951), p. 1.

6. Ibid.

7. Ibid., p. 47.

8. Ibid., pp. 48-49.

9. Neil H. Jacoby, *U.S. Aid to Taiwan* (New York: Praeger, 1966), p. 34.

10. Republic of China, Council for International Economic Cooperation and Development, *Taiwan Statistical Data Book: 1968*, Table 11-1.

11. Ibid., Table 3-7.

12. Jacoby, p. 174.

13. Ibid., p. 175.

14. *Taiwan Statistical Data Book: 1968*, Tables 5-3a, 5-4.

15. Jacoby, pp. 176-180.

16. Ibid., p. 190.

17. U.S. AID Representative, *Fifteen Years of U.S. Economic Assistance to the Republic of China* (Taipei, Taiwan: Office of the U.S. AID Representative, September 1966).

18. *Taiwan Statistical Data Book: 1968*, Table 11-7.

19. Jacoby, pp. 48-49.

20. Ibid., p. 37.

21. Chen Cheng, *Land Reform in Taiwan* (Taiwan: China Publishing Co., 1961), p. xiii.

22. Jacoby, pp. 46-47.

23. Ibid., p. 66.

24. Tillman Durdin, "G.I.'s Find Taipei Nice Spot to Visit," *New York Times*, August 10, 1967, p. 10.

25. U.S., Embassy of the United States, Taipei, Taiwan, Republic of China, *The Taiwan Economy: 1958-66 Basic Data* (Taipei: February 13, 1967), p. 8. (Mimeographed.)

26. U.S., Department of Commerce, Bureau of International Commerce, "World Trade Outlook," *International Commerce,* Vol. 73, No. 32 (August 7, 1967), p. 30.

27. *Taiwan Statistical Data Book: 1968*, Table 10-11.

28. Selwyn Feinstein, "Publishers on Taiwan Increase Their Sales of 'Pirated' Books," *Wall Street Journal*, May 29, 1967, p. 1.

29. U.S., International Cooperation Administration, *Investment Guaranty Handbook* (Washington, D.C.: Government Printing Office, n.d.).

30. Lawrence B. Krause, and Kenneth W. Dam, *Foreign Tax Treatment of Foreign Income* (Washington, D.C.: The Brookings Institution, 1964), p. 11.

31. Ibid., p. 33.

32. Ibid., pp. 35-36.

33. Ibid., p. 38.

34. Marina Von Neumann Whitman, *Government Risk-Sharing in Foreign Investment* (Princeton, N.J.: Princeton University Press, 1965), p. 51.

35. U.S., Department of Commerce, Bureau of International Commerce, *Principal Features of the China Trade Act* (Washington, D.C.: December 15, 1965). (Mimeographed.)

36. U.S., *Internal Revenue Code of 1954*, Section 941.

37. Ibid., Section 943.

3   Private American Investment in Taiwan

Investment Incentives and Promotion

The Republic of China, in order to attract foreign capital, has enacted three laws to provide suitable incentives. These are the Statute for Investment by Foreign Nationals, enacted on July 14, 1954, and amended on December 14, 1959; the Statute for Investment by Overseas Chinese, enacted on January 19, 1955, and amended on March 26, 1960; and the Statute for Encouragement of Investment, enacted on September 10, 1960, and amended on January 4, 1965.

The main incentive features of these legislative acts to attract foreign capital are as follows:

1. A newly formed corporation is exempt from income tax for a period of five years from the date on which it begins to market its products or to render services.

2. The maximum rate of corporate income tax shall not exceed 18 percent.

3. Investments in productive machinery and/or equipment and other reinvested earnings are excluded from taxable income in an amount up to 25 percent of taxable income during the year in which such investments are made.

4. A gain from the sale of securities, if they are held at least one year, is excludable from taxable income; a loss may be deducted from taxable income.

5. A tax-excluded reserve for foreign exchange loss in connection with purchase of productive equipment may be made in an amount up to 7 percent of the purchase cost.

6. Assets may be revalued when inflation, as measured by the Taipei wholesale price index, exceeds the previous valuation by 25 percent.

7. Export business transactions shall be exempt from business tax, and a deduction from taxable income of 2 percent of earnings derived from export sales is allowed.

8. Import duties on domestically unavailable productive equipment and/or machinery may be waived for companies engaged in certain industries (i.e., electronics, basic metals, petrochemicals, and others) if the company has initial total paid-up capital of $2,250,000.

9. Accelerated depreciation rates are allowed for renovated machinery and/or equipment.

10. Capital may be repatriated starting two years after investment and in the form in which invested, up to 15 percent per year.

11. Income may be repatriated without limit.

12. In the event of expropriation, an investor who holds less than 51 percent of the total capital of the enterprise may convert in foreign exchange all compensation.

13. If the investor holds more than 51 percent of the total capital, the enterprise will not be subject to expropriation for twenty years.[1]

In addition to features that offer tax benefits, protection against foreign exchange loss, waiver of import duties, repatriation of income and capital, and assurance of nonexpropriation, the Chinese government, through the Council for International Economic Cooperation and Development and particularly through a special government agency, the Investment Services Division, provides services to potential industrial investors.

Under a development program, sites were designated for industrial use. Utilities, services, and in some instances factory shells are available at each site. A free-trade zone, the Kaohsiung Export Processing Zone, with industrial facilities was opened in late 1966.

To be approved, enterprises have to be needed in Taiwan and should aid in the country's development. Preference is given to production of goods for export or for replacement of imports. The intent is to protect and nurture the development of indigenous industry and to eliminate industrial categories from overseas that will thwart or restrain the development of local enterprise.

The Council for International Economic Cooperation and Development has an office in New York that actively promotes investment opportunities by arranging efficient itineraries for visits of potential investors to Taiwan; distributes meaningful literature; solicits the attention of potential investors to the advantages of a Taiwan operation; and in conjunction with aid from overseas Chinese persons and organizations, conducts informative meetings.[2]

The preceding discussion has pertained to investments in active productive enterprises, not to portfolio investments. For purchase and/or sale of Taiwanese securities as portfolio investments, foreign nationals must obtain approval from the Ministry of Economic Affairs. Dividends and interest may not be remitted abroad until the investor has owned the securities for at least two years. Capital gains from such investment may not be remitted. The American Embassy, in noting these restrictions for portfolio investments, says they are believed to be the result of apprehension that "opening the local security market to foreign investors might provoke a large inflow of funds," thereby causing instability.[3]

Notwithstanding this attitude toward security investment, the Republic of China vigorously seeks private foreign capital.

The capital may be brought to Taiwan in the form of foreign currency or exchange; machinery, equipment, or raw materials for investor's productive use; local currency proceeds from the sale of permissible imported commodities to finance plant construction or for use as working capital; technical know-how or patent rights; principal, net profit, interest, or any other income from investment that has been approved for outward remittance in foreign exchange.[4]

Foreign Investment in Taiwan

What has been the result of these inducements? As of June 1969, foreign investment in Taiwan in the amount of $505 million has been made or approved.[5]

The bulk of foreign investments have been made by the United States, Japan, and overseas Chinese. The American investments are not as numerous but are larger than those from other sources and represent 42 percent of the overseas funds invested or approved for investment.[6]

Initially, the stress was placed by the Chinese government upon promotion of labor-intensive processing industries that produced goods required in Taiwan. This provided jobs and also substituted for imports. The textile industry is a prime example of this type of industry. As economic development progressed, it became desirable to broaden the industrial base and the emphasis has shifted to industries that require high technology and are capital intensive. This includes the petrochemical and the precision-instruments industries.

The unrest in Hong Kong in the summer of 1967 boosted the attractiveness of investment in Taiwan and other Asian countries, such as the Republic of South Korea. While relocation of going enterprises has not taken place, the belief is that second plants and also many new plants that might otherwise have located in Hong Kong have been situated elsewhere.

The wave of anti-Chinese discrimination that has taken place in Indonesia, the Philippines, and Malaysia since late 1965 has stimulated the investment in Taiwan of funds from Chinese living in those countries.

The Kaohsiung Export Processing Zone, a customs-free enclave in the harbor of the second largest city in Taiwan, was established to attract foreign companies eager to use the low-cost, competent labor on the island but interested in production solely for export markets. The Zone opened in October 1966. Ten months later, in August 1967, 26 companies were in operation in the Zone, representing an investment of $3.8 million, with 4,000 workers employed, and exporting at a $3.37 million annual rate. Many additional applications to operate in the Zone have been approved.[7]

Taiwan's success in attracting foreign capital and her program for doing so have inspired competition in the Far East. The Philippines and the Republic of Korea have recently established export-processing zones patterned on the Kaohsiung example. Other activities to attract foreign capital are also being carried out by these countries and by Malaysia.

In addition to increased economic competition, there is evidence of increased collaboration. In recognition of the limited markets that Taiwan and South Korea represent by themselves and of the efficiencies that could be achieved from productive facilities in certain capital-intensive industries on the scale of their combined markets, a Sino-Korean economic conference, held in May 1966, resulted in an agreement to explore the feasibility of joint industrial projects. Plans were made to remove trade barriers between the two countries, and construction of a nylon-making plant with productive capacity sufficient to meet the projected combined market requirements of Taiwan and South Korea has been tentatively scheduled.

The rate of foreign investment of Taiwan is increasing, and the potential for continued overseas interest appears good because of the political stability vis-à-vis Hong Kong, the continual improvements in the investment-incentive programs, and the expanded Taiwan market, which may include South Korea if this is economically advantageous.

Dimensions of American Investment in Taiwan

That U.S. industry has been responsive to business opportunity in Taiwan is borne out by the fact that through September 1967, 91 United States companies applied for and received approval from the Taiwan government to invest $121.5 million.[8]

A list of the major industries represented by these companies is as follows: electronics; pharmaceuticals; chemicals and petrochemicals; toys; banking; machinery; sewing machines; radio and television sets; lubricating-oil production. THe paucity of Taiwan's natural resources precludes mining and extractive activities, one of the principal areas of American corporate investment in most developing countries.

The American share of total foreign capital invested in Taiwan through September 30, 1967, is 58 percent. Japanese and overseas Chinese investors account for almost all of the balance. Japanese corporate interest is most prominent in the electrical and pharmaceutical industries. Overseas Chinese have mostly invested in small scale ventures, such as the hotel industry. The American companies with interests in Taiwan are predominately big corporations, including 19 of Fortune's top 500.[9]

Scope of Empirical Study

Interviews were requested from 24 corporations with reported activity in Taiwan and were granted by 20.

The 24 corporations were deemed to be representative of all companies with interests in Taiwan. Of the four companies that did not grant interviews, two said their plans were not sufficiently advanced to have anything meaningful to say; the third company advised that their president, the only person with authority to answer questions of the sort posed, was almost continuously traveling throughout the world and was unavailable; and the fourth company stated that it is against its policy to make any disclosures regarding their business activities. The last company is not publicly held and hence is probably unused to the routine requests for information to which listed American companies have become accustomed.

Twenty-eight questionnaires were mailed to companies other than those interviewed. Ten were completed and returned; two more were partially completed and returned; four additional companies disclosed that they had merely submitted applications for investment but had not made firm plans to proceed; 11 companies refused to supply information for various reasons (including eight companies which did not reply).

As the questionnaire was rather lengthy, and the questions asked were of necessity intrusive, it is felt that the response rate was satisfactory. As a yardstick of questionnaire response from corporations for a similar survey, in a study conducted at the University of Oregon in 1958, of 115 questionnaires mailed, 52 usable responses were obtained.[10] This response rate does not differ markedly from that obtained in this study.

The majority of the 30 companies with interests in Taiwan from whom information was obtained have numerous overseas ventures, as is the case with most American companies with international interests. The activity in Taiwan is just one of many. They are large companies with complex organizational structures. Nevertheless, the Taiwan operation is quite significant for at least one quarter of the companies; for two firms it is the sole foreign investment; and for three others it is the largest, and virtually the only foreign operation.

As an indicator of size, 21 of the 30 companies are publicly held and listed on the New York Stock Exchange and one is listed on the American Stock Exchange. Two investor organizations are banks, and three are privately owned companies. Only two companies may be considered to be small.

Generally, administration of the Taiwan activity is assumed by an international division or autonomous international subsidiary, which directs overseas operations for all product lines. There may be further geographical subdivisions within the international organization, for Latin America, Eastern Hemisphere, East Asia, etc. Less common, but in effect at several large companies, is an organization broken down by product lines, without distinction made between domestic and international operations. Several major companies are revamping their organization in this manner.

While operational administration is therefore decentralized, much of the specialized expertise remains on a corporate-staff level. These specialists may include lawyers, economists, and financial analysts.

Nature of Empirical Study

Interviews were held with a diversity of corporate executives. The interviewees ran the gamut from line generalists to staff specialists, from middle to upper management, and from persons with a wealth of interest and experience in Taiwan and the Far East to those with rather superficial and limited knowledge of the region.

Areas of special competence on the part of interviewees included law, finance, engineering, marketing, and administration. Often several executives were available to discuss subjects that fell within their area of competence. On several occasions, interviewees were cooperative about matters in their own field but declined to comment about matters of which they had little knowledge. Two engineers, for example, were disinclined to touch upon tax aspects but were quite eager to discuss the industrial technology involved in their Taiwan project.

What was the degree of interest in and knowledge of the Taiwan scene among corporate executives, to whom the Taiwan operation is often only a minor, peripheral matter? In general, the interviewees were men with significant and broad responsibilities in their company's international operations and had made frequent trips to or had resided for many years in the Far East.

To indicate the diversity of job function and perspective toward Taiwan, the specific titles of the key executives (but not additional staff specialists) at the twenty companies at which interviews were conducted are given:

1. General Counsel. Former AID officer in Taiwan; makes frequent trips to Far East for negotiations and inspections; familiar with Chinese history, politics, and literature.

2. Vice-President—Engineering Projects. Born and educated in China; in United States only for past fifteen years or so; makes frequent trips to Taiwan.

3. Manager—International Engineering. Has worldwide responsibilities; although has made several trips to Taiwan, has no particular knowledge of or interest in his company's Taiwan operation.

4. Vice-President—International Division. Has made numerous trips to Taiwan; although has worldwide responsibilities, is well informed and interested in the political structure of the Republic of China; is acquainted with many Chinese governmental leaders.

5. Vice-President—Administration. Background and experience in agronomy; helped establish Taiwan operation as resident manager during initial period; makes frequent long trips to Taiwan; well informed and interested in Taiwan developments.

6. Vice-President—Development, International Operation and Development Department. Economist, to whom the activity in Taiwan, while important, is only one of many similar operations in the world.

7. Vice-President—Operating Services, International Division. Former resident in charge of company's operations, first in Shanghai and then in Taiwan; sales-engineering experience.

8. General Manager—Far East. Makes frequent trips and has special responsibility for the area; major interest is in sales and distribution matters.

9. Treasurer. Although involved in decision-making that led to establishment of a Taiwan operation, it is of peripheral concern to him.

10. Manager, Licensee Operation. Engineer; has made two trips to Taiwan; essentially concerned with technical matters.

11. General Manager, Overseas Licenses and Technical Services. Has worldwide responsibilities, no special interest in Taiwan.

12. Assistant to the President of the International Division. Residence and managerial experience in Middle East and South Asia; not in Taiwan and Far East.

13. Manager, Sales Financing and Planning, International Division. Has made numerous trips to Taiwan since 1967; aware of political and economic aspects that may affect company production costs.

14. Assistant to the Chairman, Far East Division. Primary interest in company procedures and ways of doing business; no special interest in Taiwan but broad awareness of project aspects.

15. Vice-President—International Division. Despite worldwide responsibilities, quite knowledgeable and interested in Taiwan.

16. Corporate Secretary and Manager—New York Office. Prior to present assignment was company representative in Taiwan for two years; quite interested in Taiwanese matters.

17. President. Personally made all investment decisions and arrangements for his company's Taiwan venture.

18. Vice-President—International Division. Former export sales manager who set up company distributorship in Taiwan; has made many trips to Taiwan in the past two decades.

19. Vice-President—International Division. Investigated and established Taiwan operation with discretionary authority from company management.

20. Vice-President and Corporate Secretary—International Division. Lawyer; has made many trips to Taiwan; familiar with Chinese law and culture. Keen interest in Taiwan venture.

Respondents to the questionnaires could not always be identified by title, as different individuals may have answered questions in their respective areas of responsibility. The respondents' perspective toward Taiwan could not be gauged by mail.

At least half of the executives concerned with their company's venture in Taiwan seemed to have a special interest and knowledge of Taiwan. This scope and depth of interest, which may apply to many other overseas areas as well as Taiwan, may be a key reason for these men's gravitation toward, and assignment in, the international field.

Interestingly (but certainly inconclusively), the executives responsible for sole licensing but not direct investment activity seemed to regard Taiwan as just one more licensing activity. A licensing activity necessitates only minimal involvement in the affairs of the licensee country.

Corporate Overseas Investment Policies

A specific question asked of all interviewees but not included in the questionnaire because of the complexity of response was, "What are the corporate criteria for overseas investments?"

The response is indicated in Table 4.

Increased profits may consist of a vague evaluation of a specific project, as with one company, or tangibly reflect a "satisfactory" percentage return on investment on a discounted cash-flow basis. Most companies use a measure of return on investment on a discounted basis to reflect the present value of future cash as a yardstick for overseas-investment decision-making. It is generally used flexibly, in that the perceived risk will influence the required return before an investment will be made. For example, Algeria, considered a high-risk country, would have to yield a much higher rate of return than a similar investment in Costa Rica, considered a low-risk country.

Market potential includes not only the present and projected size of the market for a particular product but also its rate of growth.

Many companies have minimum-scale levels. If a project is too small it may be deemed undeserving of management attention.

For the most part, large corporations have economic-feasibility yardsticks. The fixed costs of a plant below a certain production level may be disproportionately high and force a selling price which may be vulnerable to domestic or external competition or overpriced for potential purchasers. Companies therefore undertake market studies to determine if the market growth rate will justify construction of an economically scaled production facility. Demographic, economic, social, and political factors bearing upon present and future product usage are assessed. As the length of time a plant may be under-utilized while the market is

Table 4

Major Reasons for Investing or Licensing Overseas

Reason	Number of Times Mentioned[a]
Increased profits	10
Good market potential	8
Preservation of existing market	5
Lower production costs	3
Accommodation of domestic customers	2
Availability of competent local management	1
Ease of doing business	1

[a]Some respondents gave more than one reason.

growing represents a postponement and reduction of the return of investment, the rate of market growth is a prime yardstick.

To preserve the existing market from competition, often domestic producers enjoying lower production costs and able to underprice imports, or to escape high tariff impositions, which serve to bar imports, companies may elect to invest in a local plant and partly ignore return on investment and/or market-potential factors.

Lower production costs was the basic concern of companies who assemble electronic and computer components, primarily for sale to the United States market. This is a labor-intensive operation, with lightweight, easy-to-ship subcomponents and assembled units. High labor cost and turnover in the United States have made these companies vulnerable to foreign competition, especially from Japan. Assembly abroad (so-called offshore sourcing) has been an answer. Primary concern is for steady, low-cost labor that is able to perform the delicate assembly job with meticulousness and patience. Efficient air and sea transportation service to the United States is also important.

Accommodation of domestic customers was the primary raison d'etre of the international operations of two American banks. The banks do not pioneer in market development. Rather, as a significant number of present or potential corporate customers become active in an area of the world, the major banks may establish a presence so as to be able to provide financial service. Profits, while certainly welcomed, are a secondary consideration for bank investment. The key yardstick would be the number and size of American corporations with operations in a country.

Availability of competent local management was voiced as important by one company, which believes the best and quickest way to enter a foreign market is to buy out an existing local business firm that may be in need of financial support. A factor in such acquisition would be the quality and outlook of indigenous management. Political and local-market know-how are the objectives sought.

Ease of doing business was mentioned by one company, which cited recent difficult experiences in certain other countries as situations they will seek to avoid in the future.

While increased profits are, of course, the core reason for American corporate expansion overseas, some companies take long-term views, based upon market potential, whereas others are primarily concerned with current opportunity. As greater profits can be a function of decreased costs as well as of increased sales, investment opportunity may assume different form. Political stability was constantly mentioned as a factor without which an investment will not be undertaken.

Overseas Product-Line Policies

Some companies have policies with regard to the product lines they will manufacture and/or market overseas. One drug company sets no limit upon product categories it may make and sell abroad. For this company, if there is a local need close afield to that served domestically, the product category may be entered. Products may also be tailored to conform to local usage.

As examples of this policy, the company went into the animal-feed business in Nigeria, and only in that country, as a vehicle through which to sell their animal-feed supplement. In France, a common means of taking medicants is by suppository. The company produces products in this form specifically for the French market.

This approach is perhaps an extreme. Most American companies sell abroad only the product categories that it manufactures and sells in the United States, and usually not all of them.

A chemical company, explaining that it confines itself overseas to the product categories made and sold domestically, indicates that this is because the source of technical know-how is in the United States. The company does not have any significant research and development facilities overseas.

Other companies point out that in order to assess the ease of doing business and to uncover unforeseen problems before they make substantial investments in a country, licensing operations or token investments in product categories that are not capital-intensive may be undertaken.

When an assembly operation is established overseas to serve the U.S. market, the items to be produced are clearly limited to those that have high unit value, are lightweight, and are easily shipped, so as to justify the cost of air shipment of parts and assembled units from and back to the United States. Labor as a major cost component is also a key factor. As a result of these requirements, the companies that avail themselves of offshore sourcing are commonly those in the electronic and computer industries.

Inasmuch as these are industries that are involved in fields with rapid technological change, product obsolescence is a consideration. One company executive points out that items to be produced overseas should be beyond a developmental stage but should not have "topped out" and be on the decline. This same executive also emphasized that the market in the United States for items produced overseas should be of sufficient size to justify the increased pipeline (goods-in-transit) volume.

Consumer-products manufacturers have a considerably different outlook toward the variety of products produced overseas. The product lines reflect those items for which there is a local market demand. An executive of a petrochemical company said he wished his company would emulate to some extent the approach of consumer-goods manufacturers. He would like to assess the marketability of product lines by initially manufacturing and marketing overseas on a small scale as a test of feasibility.

Selection of products for overseas ventures is related closely to the prime-profitability motive. A company with diverse product lines will not consider overseas ventures for its products with low profit margins.

The sheer size and organizational structure of a company may influence its choice of product lines for overseas ventures. One company, with decentralized management and autonomous divisions, in considering a foreign operation will include only those product categories that do not cross divisional lines.

Attitude Toward Joint Ventures

National policies toward joint ventures differ in that some countries require a degree of indigenous ownership of a foreign investment in their country. For example, Japan generally requires that the foreign share of any venture in Japan shall not exceed 50 percent. Many other countries have similarly stringent requirements. On the other hand, many nations have no restriction upon the degree of alien control. American companies, too, differ in their outlook toward joint ventures, depending on the legal restrictions involved.

The policies of the interviewed companies when the company does not have governmental restrictions to consider are outlined in Table 5.

The division of response, with half the companies wanting majority control, at least initially, and the other half willing to be minority participants is reflective of the diversity of attitude.

In general (and these judgments are based upon a rather limited sample and must be treated accordingly), it may be said that companies with a high degree of technological know-how, those who commonly will serve substantial markets in addition to the host country, and large companies with substantial financial resources tend to prefer not to enter into joint relationships and do so only when there is some peculiar advantage.

The danger of divulgement of technical secrets, the desire to avoid arguments that might arise from different ways of doing business, and the possible conflict of long-term versus short-term objectives were cited as reasons for not wanting to yield a voice in operating policy to minority interests. Specifically mentioned by three companies were instances where minority interests wanted an early payout of dividends and the American companies preferred to retain earnings so as to provide for future growth (and although not mentioned, incidentally postpone payment of U.S. income taxes). Arguments over higher-than-expected start-up costs were also mentioned.

The two companies that prefer complete ownership initially, with dilution later through the sale of stock, felt that the initial dividend and other operating patterns would then have been established and areas of potential conflict would be minimal. Furthermore, sale of equity would not necessarily reduce operating control if the stock is sold to a number of different local people with purely investment concern. Before the securities may be underwritten, it is beneficial to have a "track-record" of satisfactory operating results and earnings, in order to encourage purchase. Hence, an initial period of time is desirable during which the companies maintain complete control and successfully launch the enterprise.

While a basic question asked by companies wanting to maintain at least majority control was, "What can the partner contribute?," several of the companies that favored joint ventures supplied answers. Local know-how, in terms of ability to obtain labor and

Table 5

Attitude Toward Joint Ventures

Preference	Number of companies
100 percent ownership on continuing basis	6
100 percent ownership initially, then dilute	2
Majority interest	2
Minority interest	3
License arrangement	2
No preference	5
Total companies	20

raw materials, cognizance of local customs, and acquaintance with government officials and policies, was mentioned as a prime contribution of an indigenous partner. It was also felt by several companies that a local partner represents an additional safety factor for the investment.

Two companies mentioned a moral obligation, acquired in the evolution of their overseas ventures from sales through distribution to establishment of a local subsidiary. The distributor whose worthy efforts have contributed to the decision to enter the market directly is in danger of being dismissed. A minority interest is often sold to the ex-distributor, both to avoid what otherwise would be a financial blow and to provide continuity during the transition from distributorship to subsidiary operation. One joint venture was actually initiated by the distributor, who advised the American company of the investment opportunity.

Companies differ as to the percentage of ownership that constitutes effective control. Simple majority (51 percent) interest was said to be inadequate by two companies and their policy was that 60 percent and 75 percent, respectively, are necessary equity levels to insure control.

The companies who either preferred or had no objection to a role as a minority partner had a variety of reasons for their position.

Banks, whose prime reason for involvement in many overseas ventures is to accommodate their domestic corporate customers by serving their foreign needs, are concerned with the safety and sound business operation of the activity in which they have invested. They do not, however, care to participate actively in daily operations. As a consequence, enough equity to ensure a voice in management and a presence in the area is sufficient to meet the banks' objectives.

Two companies preferred to license, and one company to participate overseas as a minority interest, because of admitted lack of international experience, qualified personnel, and fear of the risks of overseas ventures. One of the company executives pointed to the different culture and economic environment and expressed the opinion that alternative investment opportunities in the United States presented far less uncertainty. This view closely matches that found by Aharoni, who points out that there is a widespread feeling among American business executives that foreign investments are risky because other countries are not like the United States.[11]

Another situation is that of a privately owned engineering firm that specializes in the design and production of textile plants. The company typically will quote a price for a going textile-manufacturing operation with guaranteed daily production of a specific fiber. The company's market is to a considerable extent centered in developing nations, where the labor intensity and the ability to substitute for imports, characteristics of the textile industry, makes it ideally suited. A key to gaining a sale is to arrange long-term financing and to obtain foreign exchange so as to enable the importation of machinery. In order to get the transaction started, this company has on quite a few occasions invested equity capital itself. The company is always in a minority position and does not get involved in operations other than engineering consultation.

The other companies who expressed no preference essentially have a flexible and pragmatic policy whereby they will participate in a venture in which they may exploit their technical know-how and experience on any profitable basis, with or without control. Such was the case where a petrochemical company was asked by the Chinese government to join with a public government corporation in building a chemical-fertilizer plant. The American company that was offered a majority interest in this venture, lacking specific product expertise and experience, solicited the participation of another American company, which had just completed construction of a similar facility in Korea. The two American companies agreed to an equal split of interest, so that the final equity division was American Company A, 35 percent; American Company B, 35 percent, and the Chinese governmental corporation had the balance of 30 percent. Neither American company had any reservation over participation with less than majority control. The inherent merits of the venture overshadowed any question as to the degree of interest. The agreement specified the functional work area and management positions that each participant would fill.

Types of Activity in Taiwan

Discussion up to now has focused upon considerations with regard to overseas ventures in general.

With specific reference to the companies with business activities in Taiwan who were either interviewed or answered questionnaires (including two partial answers), the nature of the activities are shown in Table 6.

The pattern is for companies to institute manufacturing facilities as they become experienced, through licensing sales and/or distributor arrangements, with aspects of doing business in Taiwan.

Two companies (one with a distributorship, and the other with a licensing arrangement) were actively considering an equity investment in a manufacturing operation. Five of the companies with manufacturing facilities on Taiwan had originally had a distributorship or a sales office arrangement.

The Nature of Financing

What is the source and pattern of financing of U.S. corporate activity in Taiwan? How does the debt-equity relationship compare with similar company investments domestically and overseas? And, why?

Twenty-six of the 30 companies queried report equity investments in Taiwan. The four others have licensing or distributorship arrangements with negligible, if any, capital investment. Of the 26 companies with equity investment, 12 had an all-equity investment, 14 a debt-and-equity investment. The response pertains to the initial outlay and source of finances as the activity got underway.

Of the twelve companies that reported an investment entirely of equity capital, three have relatively small operations (costing under $1 million); one company would not reveal the amount; one company had invested $1 million as a temporary measure to get the venture underway and planned to eventually withdraw its interest from the joint venture; and another company had $1.5 million of blocked local funds derived from an existing venture as a source of funds. Only one of the companies that had invested only equity funds had a sizable operation. This company invested

Table 6

Nature of Activity in Taiwan

Type	Number of companies
Manufacturing and/or assembling	23
Sales office facility	6
Distributorship	4
Licensing arrangement	5
Other	3
Total activities	41[a]

[a]Nine of the 32 companies were engaged in more than one type of activity in Taiwan.

$2.5 million and stated that future financial needs would be met by local borrowing, either at the prevailing 11 or 12 percent interest rates or at Cooley Fund rates.

These lower Cooley loans, in New Taiwan Dollars, are available to U.S. firms for business development or trade expansion in Taiwan. A factor that is weighed in deciding whether to borrow Cooley funds through a loan from the Export-Import Bank is the requirement to buy American machinery and equipment. Several companies have decided that higher interest rates are preferable to this Cooley loan stipulation.

The $2.5 million investment mentioned above closely matched the "magic" $2,250,000 minimum capital investment level set by the Republic of China as a requirement to gain exemption from duty on imported machinery and equipment. Companies with offshore sourcing operations find it essential to avoid duty payments on the inflow of components for assembly.

The large majority of companies had borrowed mostly local funds to complement their equity capital. This is a common practice in overseas investment, as American corporations seek to minimize risk to invested capital. Despite the often high interest expense, this maneuver is economically sound because it cushions the impact of a possible freeze of repatriability of capital, host-country obstruction, and other contingencies. It is also a hedge against inflation and devaluation of currency, as the loans are for fixed amounts and interest rates. Availability of local funds as a source of borrowing is sometimes a key factor in investment decisions. Borrowing may also be made from the United States.

In Taiwan, where repatriation of capital is limited to the amount of 15 percent annually after two years of operation, there is no restriction upon repayment of loans. Also, as the required minimum paid-in capital of $2,250,000 (for duty-exempt importation) pertains to initial investment, a company may repatriate its capital over a period of years, as permitted, at the same time maintaining its outstanding debt. In essence, if could operate eventually (in nine years) entirely with borrowed funds, if the lender did not require equity capital to be kept in the business.

This strategy, although advantageous to American corporate interests, was the cause of a disagreement with a Chinese corporate partner in one reported case. While the American company wished to declare and repatriate dividends from earnings, the Chinese firm wished to apply earnings to debt reduction, so as to lower the burden of high interest expense. Also, to the American partner, who probably would incur imposition of an aggregate Chinese and American income tax of up to 48 percent upon repatriated earnings, interest expense could be viewed benevolently, as in actuality the governmental authorities would bear the brunt of almost half of the interest expense. The Chinese partner, on the other hand, with a maximum corporate income tax of only 18 percent, does not have the same motivation to seek tax deductions rather than cost reductions.

One company spokesman expressed the observation that the high leverage provided by borrowed funds is most beneficial when the business is going well, but should there be a downturn, as occurred to a subsidiary of his corporation in Latin America recently, the difficulties are compounded.

The debt-equity ratios of the 14 companies reporting this arrangement are presented in Table 7.

The variance in debt-equity ratios seems to be a function of the required minimum paid-in capital requirement and the size of the total capital expenditure. With regard to the latter consideration, the larger the operation, the more eager the participant company to minimize and spread risk by borrowing.

Generally, companies reported higher debt-equity ratios overseas than domestically, with Taiwan following the customary pattern. The two partner companies with a 9:1 ratio departed considerably from their usual overseas pattern. One of the companies indicated that its usual debt-equity ratio overseas is 2:1. One interviewee expressed skepticism about the future repatriability of capital as statutorily permitted. He pointed out that the Foreign Exchange Control Board must give permission in specific cases, and in the event of a future squeeze on foreign-exchange reserves, the Board would quite logically suspend the privilege. This was a key reason for his company's maintaining a "thin" equity balance and supplementing the equity with borrowed U.S. funds.

Table 7

Percentage Debt-Equity Financing of Capital Expenditures
Reported by U.S. Corporations

Company	Total capital expenditure	U.S. equity	U.S. loans	Local loans	
1	$ 8,000,000	10%	90%	—	Companies 1 and 2 are partners with a 70 percent share of the venture. A Chinese company with local funds has 30 percent interest.
2	8,000,000	10%	90%	—	
3	12,000,000	45%	—	55%	Whether Cooley funds will be used is undecided.
4	600,000	42%	—	58%	Local borrowing in Cooley Funds.
5	20,000,000	33%	—	67%	Local borrowing in Cooley Funds.
6	4,150,000	56%	—	—	Ratio is function of $2.3 million equity to obtain duty-free parts importation. Source of loans not reported.
7	11,000,000	27%	—	—	Source of loans not reported.
8	—	—	—	—	No figures divulged.
9	2,250,000	—	—	—	No figures divulged, but equity is at least $2,250,000 and their borrowing was reported as from the United States.
10	2,300,000	87%	—	—	Source of loans not reported.
11	100,000	50%	—	50%	Local borrowing.
12	1,000,000	—	—	—	No figures divulged, but use of Cooley Funds reported.
13	—	—	—	—	Companies 13 and 14 are partners. No figures divulged, but local borrowing reported at "around 50%."
14	—	—	—	—	

Future Financing Needs, Disposition of Earnings, and Implications

While judgments as to future financing plans are quite tentative, since, for the most part, activity is just getting under way, expectations serve to reflect corporate investor attitudes.

What are these expectations? For one thing, initial capital took the form of machinery, parts, and technical know-how, as well as funds. Future needs will lean more to working capital.

The imponderable of United States policy with regard to the balance of payments problem raises the probability that there will be continued pressure to repatriate earnings in the form of dividends.

The economic climate in the United States is also a consideration. For example, periods of tight money and a faltering stock market (which would discourage underwriting) could lead to an increased flow of dividends from overseas to help finance domestic needs. Current United States tax laws further encourage this homeward flow, since taxes may be levied against overseas earnings whether repatriated or not.

On the other hand, and pertaining to repatriation of capital and not to earnings, the terms of loans from both AID and the Export-Import Bank require that some capital remain in the host company operation over the life of the loans.

Only three companies of those interviewed reported their intent to repatriate capital. Several spokesmen stressed, however, that if there was danger that they would not be able to repatriate capital, then they probably would. The three companies that plan to repatriate initial capital expect to substitute retained earnings, which would be subject to less restriction as to repatriability, for future financial needs.

A common outlook was that the investment could be most expeditiously recovered through a dividend policy that repatriated earnings as quickly as generated. One company pointed to the investment incentive that permits a tax-deductible reserve to be set up, to meet contingent foreign-exchange loss in connection with equipment purchase, as a partial source of future financing. The company pointed out that in some countries in which they had operations they perceived local sensitivities to be offended by the continued outpouring of profits to the United States. In several countries stock in the subsidiaries was sold locally as a means to mollify feelings. This represents the long-term approach to doing business overseas, as opposed to the short-term—seeking to expatriate capital as well as earnings as quickly as possible.

Perhaps the prime exponent of a long-term approach was a director of international operations who said,

> Today our capital, technological knowledge and experience, and willingness to take risks is wanted by developing countries such as Taiwan. But what will the attitude be in 15 years, when they don't need us and all they see are profits being sent back to the United States? We are in business for the long pull. We want to be good citizens of the countries in which we do business. If the country is in a foreign-exchange bind we will not repatriate earnings.
>
> The only thing that guards against expropriation of going concerns is the desire for additional investment. It is the intention of my company to sell to Chinese people 50 percent or more stock interest in the Taiwan subsidiary. A dividend policy that takes into consideration the Government's foreign exchange position at any time will be necessary. A dividend policy will also be necessary because the investors will be relatively unsophisticated and will rely upon dividend yield, rather than earnings yardsticks.
>
> This would be the first foreign company to make a stock offering in Taiwan. There is a question as to how much stock the public can absorb. The price will be a problem. We will probably set it at about 20 percent below its assessed valuation. [Setting the price of a new stock issue below its assessed value is standard procedure in the United States. It is done in order to help insure a successful underwriting, and to build confidence in the security during the early years because there will be more likelihood that the market price will go up rather than down.] Since the Taiwan currency is stable, the stock need not be viewed as a hedge as is true in some South American countries. The Company would support the stock price through open market purchases, if need be, to maintain a level of confidence.

The viewpoint expressed in this interview departs from the usual practice of "multinational" corporations (a term considered by many government leaders and local businessmen to be a euphemism for American corporate entities), who offer the "opportunity" to nationals of the host country to acquire stock in the parent company although local interests identify only with the indigenous subsidiary. The host country's anxiety about potential economic upset (a multinational corporate group may at any point decide that cost advantages or other benefits are more attractive elsewhere and relocate their operation to another country) is unallayed by absentee control or extremely fractional local equity interest in the parent company. The questions of jurisdictional control and conflicting interests also plague the relations between nation-states and multinational corporations. One observer expects this relationship to remain stormy for a long time.[12]

The contemplated action of the above company to sell majority ownership of the indigenous subsidiary to local interests is unquestionably a step in the direction of international business/foreign governmental harmony. The corporation would, of course, have to assess the sacrifice of a portion of profits and abdication of that area of managerial decision-making that extends to relocation of subsidiaries and other extranational actions against a return of greater security from expropriation; acquisition of capital derived from the sale of stock, which becomes available to invest profitably elsewhere; and, probably, more local cooperation and less "red tape" in matters that require governmental oversight and procedure.

Operational control need not be affected, as the sale of stock can be to a broad base of individuals with little interest in assumption of management function.

Twenty of the 40 companies questioned said that they would repatriate some dividends as earned. Ten companies, including eight of the 20, said that they would reinvest some earnings to meet the needs of the Taiwan operation. Three companies said that they would reinvest the funds internationally, either to cover losses elsewhere, or to participate in a more profitable opportunity. Seven companies either had not made a decision or did not answer this question.

It is clear that there is a wide difference in strategy with regard to expansion and improvement of the Taiwan facilities as reflected by the intended proportion of retained earnings. Judgmental calculation indicates that the percentage of retained earnings of American corporations in Taiwan will be close to that for the average of all direct American investments abroad—30 percent (1960-1966 average).[13] Indeed, the same large companies pursue the same dividend policies elsewhere in the world and largely account for this pattern.

Noneconomic Aspects of American Private Investment

Most striking in viewing the diversity of financial arrangements are the differences in attitude among American corporate leaders as regards the degree of identification of their corporate interest with that of the host countries in which they have invested their capital, time, and energy.

One American investment banker points to the substantial contribution made by private American capital to the economies of foreign countries but indicates social and political aspects of direct investment that increasingly overshadow the economic factors.[14]

The social aspects that he delineates are the following:

1. Nobody wants his nation's basic industries to be controlled by foreigners.

2. As local businessmen appraise potential fields for expansion, they feel excluded from areas in which American subsidiaries are engaged. The competitive gap is further increased because American subsidiaries have access to the research and development resources of the parent company.

3. The sheer size of the American subsidiaries leads to their absorption of a disproportionate share of scarce local resources.

4. Foreign executives of American subsidiaries do not have responsibility comparable to that of their American counterparts. The foreign manager customarily reports to an American director of international operations or to a lower-echelon official in the international department. The American manager will have a more abbreviated reporting relationship to top management.

He outlines the political implications as follows:

1. The parent country may have a law that conflicts with the laws of the host country. Compliance by an American subsidiary may generate cries of interference with the host country's foreign policy.

2. Action of the United States to speed American corporate repatriation of foreign earnings to improve the American balance of payments has the reciprocal effect of worsening the balance of payments in the host country.

3. Evidence or suspicion of U.S. diplomatic pressure on behalf of American companies can cause bad feeling. An example of a future problem is the planned investment of several American oil companies in refinery facilities on Okinawa, with the apparent acquiescence of the U.S. government. This has aroused Japanese concern that the investment is being made now, before the

reversion of the Ryukyus to Japan, in order to circumvent Japanese prohibition of more than 50 percent foreign ownership of corporate entities.

In the face of these criticisms and notwithstanding the substantial benefits American corporate investment has conferred upon foreign economic development, it seems clear that the national interests of both the United States and the host country and the continued security of U.S. business interests would be best served by a long-range view. This would bring the actions and policies of American-controlled branches and subsidiaries into harmony with the economic, political, and social objectives of the host company. Legislation to exempt American-controlled entities from compliance to U.S. statutes in the event of conflict with host country laws should be enacted. Perhaps the tax laws of foreign countries could provide incentive for establishment of research and development facilities on a decentralized basis. At any rate, studies should be undertaken to devise means to encourage those actions that befit the long-range view.

Form of Capital Invested in Taiwan

The form of initial paid-in capital among the 20 interviewed companies revealed considerable diversity, as shown in Table 8.

Four of the 20 companies had licensing arrangements and invested no capital.

While used machinery is ordinarily subject to duty payment, exceptions are made when the equipment is of a highly specialized nature. This was the situation for two of the three companies that brought used machinery to Taiwan. The third company transferred a manufacturing operation, including equipment, from Hong Kong after termination of a contractual arrangement there and paid the regular duty.

The technical know-how invested consisted of designs and tolerance standards, as well as salaries and allowances of technical personnel, including quality-control inspectors, during the plant start-up periods.

The Investment Decision

Corporations reported a diversity of specific motives for electing to invest in Taiwan. Initial consideration and investigation preceded the final decision.

Table 8

Form of Capital Invested

	Number of Companies
U.S. dollars	16
Local funds	7
New machinery	10
Used machinery	3
Raw materials and parts	8
Technical know-how	10

The initial consideration of a possible operation in Taiwan came about in a variety of ways, although two common factors were (1) a search for appropriate offshore sourcing sites to counter foreign competition in the United States, and (2) desire to preserve the Taiwan export market from competition.

The experience of the 20 companies interviewed may serve to illustrate the different ways in which attention came to be focused on this business opportunity.

Company	Reason for Considering a Taiwan Venture
1	Solicited by the Republic of China Government.
2	Company 1 offered this company a share in a venture in which the company had technical expertise and experience.
3	Company salesman perceived a local market opportunity in Taiwan for certain manufactured goods if produced in the country and made the suggestion to his management.
4	The Taiwan distributor of Company 4 suggested that competition for the Taiwan market could be successfully met by lower-cost local manufacture.
5	This company was the distributor for Company 4 and wanted to participate jointly in the venture that it had recommended.
6	Operates in Taiwan on a royalty basis from a licensing arrangement. This is a continuation of a former arrangement on the Chinese mainland. The company organization is highly decentralized and is structured into product groups, which handle international as well as domestic business activity, a structure that has come into being in recent years. Line management are predominately persons with domestic experience and little overseas interest. As a result, a staff manager with considerable experience and residence in the Far East expressed the view that Taiwan is perceived by division management to be obscure and remote,

whereas "glamorous" Hong Kong would be more readily acceptable as a candidate for investment.

7   This company also limits its Taiwan activity to a licensing arrangement, which also is a legacy of operations on mainland China. A different organization structure from that of Company 6 prevails, and a Far Eastern branch of the International Division exists. Presently, an additional manufacturing operation is planned for the area, but the decision as to location has not yet been made. Taiwan is a candidate.

8   The present Taiwan licensee of this company decided that its own manufactured item was inferior technically and not as salable as that produced by Company 8. By coincidence, a sales representative happened to be in Taiwan at the time of that realization, and partly due to the man's alertness to opportunity, a licensing arrangement was made.

9   The President of a Taiwan company approached Company 9 with sales-volume figures that justified a licensing arrangement for expensive machines.

10   An existing fee-basis manufacturing contract in Hong Kong was to expire at a specific early date for undisclosed reasons, and the company conducted a deliberate search in the area for a replacement location.

11   The company's sole customer on Taiwan, a government-owned corporation, decided to buy only from local producers and so notified the company.

12   This company is a bank and was invited by a group of Chinese bankers to participate in a joint venture.

13   A combination of urging by the Chinese government and the establishment of an American competitor's manufacturing plant on Taiwan led the company to evaluate the merits of an investment on the island.

14   A group consisting of officials of the Republic of China Government and private Chinese executives

asked the company to participate in a venture that would help to develop a needed industry in Taiwan.

15   This company, feeling the impact of foreign-made competitive products on its market share in the United States, undertook a deliberate search for an offshore sourcing location. Taiwan was one of many candidates throughout the world.

16   A Chinese-owned firm approached the company for technical know-how and credits and sought the company's participatory investment as an aid in securing loans.

17   This company is a worldwide enterprise, with operations in most countries in the world. It had a branch office in Taiwan and decided to convert this into a subsidiary after legal restrictions were placed upon its foreign-exchange dealings as a foreign-sales operation.

18   Taiwan had been an export market for the company. When an American competitor was reported to be investigating the possibility of building a plant in Taiwan, the company became concerned over the prospect of losing a growing market.

19   This company was similarly faced with the threat of losing Taiwan as an export market because of reported competitive action.

20   Lower-cost Japanese competition was hurting the company's volume of sales and profits in the U.S. market. The cost differential was due to the labor component, and the company conducted a deliberate search in the Far East for an offshore sourcing location.

Investigation and Recommendation

The nature of the investigation and study that followed the original interest in a Taiwan venture also varied from company to company. Approaches also differed, largely reflecting the varying complexities of organization structure and the operational plans of the different companies.

The investigations were centered upon two broad concerns. First, could the purposes for investment (i.e., offshore sourcing, sale to the Taiwan market) be reasonably achieved; that is, what would be the production costs and/or the size and growth of Taiwan market potential, etc. Second, would the specific negotiable and statutory arrangements make for a feasible investment.

Large corporations with complex operations, diffused decision-making processes, and highly specialized personnel sent a team or a continual flow of specialists to Taiwan to make on-the-spot surveys. These studies sometimes took several years to prepare. In smaller companies, which usually posed less complicated situations, highly placed executives could make evaluations and conduct negotiations without the need to assess other opportunities for corporate capital.

Large companies customarily have a standard preinvestment investigation format, accompanied by check-off lists to insure coverage of all aspects. The standardization of approach facilitates comparison with alternate investment opportunities.

The team composition varied by company, seldom by situation. The Taiwan team investigations invariably included a financial analyst (one company had an additional financial analyst, who specialized in taxes), and if Taiwan was to be the outlet for production, then a market analyst would also be present. While Chinese lawyers were retained by all companies to prepare contracts and assist in other procedural ways, members of corporate legal staffs sometimes participated. Other specialists included an oil company's China-area specialist and an agronomist from a chemical company who aided in the evaluation of market potential for chemical fertilizer through assessment of the land and of programs to educate farmers. While the specialists from each company usually traveled together as a team, one company sent the following sequence of visitors: first, a market analyst, to estimate the market size and growth rate; second, an engineer, to determine the scale of installation and magnitude of capital investment to meet the projected market requirements; third, an operations analyst, to gauge the cost of operation of a plant of specified size; and finally a real estate man, to assess land and location availabilities.

The aim of investigations, of course, is to gather facts in order to develop a recommendation. Investigators in a large company usually consider their proposals to management carefully, since a veto by management may be construed to be a personal rejection. Far more facts are generated than are actually needed for most investment decisions, and the weight of argument is usually compelling, or it is not presented.

With smaller companies, the procedure is quite different and usually faster. The President and/or Treasurer may take one or two trips and make a decision in the field as expeditiously as possible. Sometimes sales representatives in the area do the preliminary footwork.

Since investigations are costly in terms of money and time, as much prescreening as possible is done prior to travel. The Chinese Investment and Trade Office (CITO), the New York branch of the Investment Services Division, fills a key function by providing relevant information prior to field investigation and arranging itineraries and meetings with officials, so that time in Taiwan may be efficiently utilized.

In addition to CITO, which was adjudged excellent by all interviewees who had any contact with it, assistance was provided by Chinese officials in Taiwan, who helped in the selection of sites and paved the way for long-term cooperation, and by the U.S. State Department and the American Embassy in Taipei, who gave advice as to the political climate on Taiwan. The Taiwan tariff figures were a valuable guide in estimating the size of markets. One director of international operations, incidentally, made the comment that this data was much more reliable than in the Philippines, where a high rate of smuggling has distorted the meaningfulness of the figures.

Smaller companies generally relied more upon outside advice, since their staffs were usually thinly stretched. This outside aid included information from banks and private consultants situated or with experience in the Far East, U.S. Commerce Department trade data, and any other source of information that might be available. For example, one manager at a medium-sized company with a Taiwan licensing arrangement, who had little familiarity with the area, used a New York *Times* Sunday Supplement to up-date the Commerce Department information he had originally used in evaluating the Taiwan market.

A common reaction to dealing with Chinese economic-development officials was expressed by a finance executive who had been a member of an initial investigation team and had made two subsequent trips to Taiwan:

> On my very first trip I saw the Finance Minister and the Vice-President of the Republic of China. They're going all out to encourage foreign investment. The purpose is to provide jobs in the face of high unemployment and a soaring population.

Companies concerned with preservation of Taiwan's export-market sales and companies investigating licensing arrangements centered their interest on Taiwan, but other corporations, particularly those who wished to establish offshore sourcing operations, had alternate choices. What were the other choices and why were they rejected?

Since complete control and ownership is desired by companies interested in offshore sourcing operations, Japan is eliminated from competition because it requires at least 50 percent Japanese interest in foreign-investment activities.

Another consideration, political stability, is a vital factor in selection of an area for investment. Although capital may be protected by an AID guarantee, the destruction or expropriation of production facilities for essential components of finished goods could have an adverse impact on corporate earnings far greater than the value of the components themselves.

Hong Kong, after the 1967 riots, was viewed in this light.

The Republic of Korea, which followed Taiwan's lead in structuring legal codes and organizing economic-ministry personnel in order to attract foreign capital, has been remarkably successful in this regard since early 1966 and must be considered a formidable competitor of Taiwan. The Treasurer of a company which had initiated a substantial investment in Taiwan prior to 1966 stated that if the investment were being made at the time of the interview the decision might well have been in favor of South Korea. The reasons given were that South Korea had benefited from too frequent changes in program in Taiwan and had leap-frogged in an efficient way.

Okinawa, which is still occupied by American military forces and offers the most security of any Far Eastern area, has enjoyed considerable American investment interest since 1967. Coincident with a flow of American capital has been a rise of Japanese concern that the investments are intended to circumvent Japan's 50 percent ownership law by establishment of a 100 percent ownership position prior to the reversion of Okinawa to Japan, scheduled to take place in 1972. One oil company official denied that this was the intent and said that Okinawa represented an attractive site for investment. He would not speculate on the ramifications of Japanese resumption of jurisdiction over the Ryukyus.

Two companies that were interviewed weighed countries as far afield from Taiwan as Portugal as alternatives for offshore sourcing. For various reasons, largely reflecting political stability and lower-cost, efficient labor, Taiwan was selected.

Decision-Making and Start-Up

Modern American business corporations are highly complex organizations, and except for the dwindling number of larger companies in which one-man rule persists, decision-making is often by committee, after prescreening at lower hierarchic levels. It is difficult to pinpoint what circumstances or influences affected the outcome of deliberation, or the nature of the recommendation in the form in which it was finally presented for decision.

Decisions to invest essentially as recommended were made promptly in most cases. The President of one company decided to wait until the market grew to a certain "economic size," which he deemed it had reached two years later. Differences of opinion and indecision developed on the Board of Directors of one large company because the Taiwan operation entailed entering a new product field. It took eight months for an affirmative decision to be made. Interestingly, two years later the company made a major domestic acquisition of a company engaged in this new product area. A company representative credited the Taiwan experience with providing the impetus for this acquisition.

Companies who elected to invest had to apply formally to and get approval from the government of the Republic of China, acquire a site, and construct the facility. A myriad of other less significant arrangements, of course, also had to be made. Most companies complained of excessive red tape and bureaucratic procedure. Specific annoyances that were frequently mentioned were that too many copies of forms were required to be filled out because of the large number of officials who had to pass judgment, and long delays were caused by translation of documents.

Several interviewees set forth rationales for the laborious governmental procedures. One Director of International Operations said,

There was a period of bureaucratic shakeout after promulgation of the new investment incentive laws. This is no different than the situation in the United States after a tax law is passed, when there is usually a period of at least six months before the courts and regulatory agencies rule on how the law is to be interpreted and implemented. Bureaucratic delay in Taiwan is no worse than elsewhere in the world.

An interviewee who had resided in Taiwan for two years said,

There is a corps of bureaucrats on duty sufficient to handle mainland China needs should recovery ever occur. The red tape and excessive bureaucracy is due to the need to keep these men busy. Overall governmental authorities are helpful. Despite red tape they find ways to get things done—sometimes through payoffs. There is nothing really flagrant or crooked, but it helps to influence interpretation, but not violation, of laws. It's a cultural matter. The Chinese are dynamic and enormously capable.

With the exception of a few individuals who tried to be understanding, excessive red tape was pointed to as a leading cause for complaint by virtually all industrial investors interviewed. Indeed, Chinese industrial development officials acknowledged the problem and asked for patient understanding. The Director of the Investment Services Division said his organization promised to do all it could to expedite applications and other pending matters. This official facetiously told a largely American audience of established and potential investors that he had succeeded in reducing the number of required application copies so that only 36 are needed. In a more serious vein he then made a public assurance that all investment applications would be acted upon within 120 days.[15]

Despite frequent difficulties, construction time tables and cost estimates were generally met. It is possible that expectations of bureaucratic delay were built into the schedules. Nevertheless, the plans to bring operations "on stream" came to fruition.

While there was near-unanimous comment about excessive bureaucracy, one may question not its existence, but rather its seriousness. American businessmen, as Aharoni pointed out in his study, "do not have great respect for government in general, and in any less developed country he believes neither in its stability nor in its ability."[16] There is a strong predisposition against government regulation, and therefore, perhaps, when it is encountered the impact is magnified.

Reasons for Investing in Taiwan

What were the major reasons that led to recommendations and decisions to invest in Taiwan rather than alternate locations?

Twenty-six companies when personally interviewed or queried by mail gave specific reasons why they decided to invest in Taiwan.

The reasons for investment or licensing in Taiwan closely reflect the motive for the operation.

The pattern is outlined in Table 9.

As is obvious, companies that invest in a manufacturing facility in order to preserve their sales in Taiwan regard the market as attractive. Also very important to these companies, and an inducement without which most would not have invested, is the diminution of risk through government assurance that it will buy the entire output at a prescribed price. Assurance of the availability of raw materials needed for manufacture at a fixed price was also given in the case of natural gas. These government assurances eliminate any fear that the companies will not be able to market their products profitably. In order to underwrite the assurance of sales, the privilege to produce a specific item is usually granted to one company only, and in essence constitutes a legal monopoly. The company in return has to construct a facility of sufficient scale to produce 100 percent of the island's needs for that product or an agreed-upon quantity.

One international division Vice-President, although pleased with the noncompetitive arrangement, pointed out that in the Central American Common Market a similar privilege is granted but companies have to provide only 50 percent of the market requirements.

Table 9

Reasons for Selection of Taiwan

Reason	Primary reasons for company overseas venture						
	Offshore sourcing	Taiwan market	Licensing	Banks	Produce for export	Facilitate sale	Total[a]
Attractive market		11	2	1			14
Minimal risk		7	1		1		9
Low-cost labor	5	1			1		7
Political and economic stability	2	3	1				6
Preserve export market		6					6
Profitability		4			1		5
Government attitude and business climate	3	1		1			5
Physical facilities	2				2		4
Local management talent	1				2		3
Incentives	1				1		2
Chance to export		1					1
Chance to be first		1					1
Advantages of China Act		1					1
Gain sales						1	1
Serve U.S. customers				1			1

[a]Several companies gave more than one reason.

While Taiwan benefits through the entry of foreign capital, more jobs, and exchange, the Taiwanese consumer, in paying higher prices than he would in a competitive market situation, is subsidizing the arrangements. While the companies are quite receptive to the low-risk situation, one company Vice-President expressed the reservation that the high cost of raw materials (which is also government established) in turn necessitated the admittedly high price of his company's product. The high government-established prices of products render companies unable to export from Taiwan because they cannot meet competitive prices elsewhere.

Several of the present fixed price and assured market arrangements are for specific periods of time, subject to renegotiation and agreement. Other arrangements implicitly place a duty upon the companies to expand their facilities as the market needs expand, so that they continue to furnish 100 percent of Taiwan's requirements.

The other reasons for corporate activity in Taiwan appeared to reflect directly the companies' specific interests. Offshore-sourcing companies are particularly interested in trainable, low-cost labor and a cooperative and receptive government attitude that minimizes the risk of disruption to their production schedules.

Dimension of Operation

Only one company, involved in an offshore-sourcing operation, reported that its Taiwan facility was large relative to its facilities in the United States and elsewhere. Generally, the smaller scale of the Taiwan facility is a reflection of the relatively small size of the Taiwan market; for offshore-sourcing companies, the activity is primarily an assembly operation.

Another specific consideration is the advance of technology, which relates to plant size in certain product fields. For example, an ammonia plant constructed in Taiwan in 1961 has a daily output of 320 tons, within the normal range for such plants at that time. In 1967, as a result of technological advances, the range of output for new plants was 600 to 1,500 tons of ammonia daily. The Taiwan ammonia plant is, therefore, small relative to the plants the company currently constructs.

Table 10

Employment Pattern of 24 Companies

Company activity	Number employees and predominate skill involved	Number resident Americans
1. Synthetic fiber manufacture. Minority interest in Chinese-controlled and -managed company.	Several thousand; manual dexterity for machine operating.	None (several engineers were present during the start-up period).
2. Manufacture of processing equipment through subcontractors. Provides engineering services to subcontractors. Joint venture of two U.S. companies.	Small staff of Chinese chemical and mechanical engineers. (Subcontractors must have skilled labor.)	None.
3. Manufacture of polyethylene in capital-intensive operation that converts naphtha to solid polyethylene pellets, which are then sold to plastic extruders.	Several hundred; dial-watching and trouble-shooting.	One, the General Manager, who is an American of Chinese descent.
4. Production of urea and ammonia from natural gas. Output sold as fertilizer or base for plastic extrusion. Three-company venture (two U.S. corporations and one Chinese publicly owned corporation).	323 workers, including supervisors. Machine maintenance, dial-watching, manual labor to bag the output. (Operation is capital-intensive.)	Two.
5. Offshore sourcing of television tuners, complex capacitors and a wide variety of electronic parts and components.	3,500 in late 1967, 4,000 expected in 1968; manual dexterity and skill in testing.	Six.
6. Manufacture of batteries for worldwide export.	160; engineering with battery experience, careful workmanship.	None.
7. Offshore sourcing of transistors and assembly of memory cores for computers.	Number not disclosed; meticulous weaving of thousands of wires (mostly female employees).	Not disclosed.
8. Manufacture of plasticizers for sale to local polyvinylchloride manufacturers.	150; dial-watching, trouble-shooting, engineering.	6 Americans initially, "in ten years—none."

9. Sales and sales engineering of business machines, from typewriters to electronic data processing equipment.	55; selling, sales engineering, repairing and servicing, clerical skills.	None.
10. Extrusion of plastics.	Not reported.	None.
11. Manufacture of cigarette filters utilizing patented process, for sale to government tobacco monopoly.	12-15; machine operating.	None.
12. Tabletizing and encapsulating bulk antibiotic mixture for sale to Taiwan market.	66 (includes 32 in production who manipulate bulk); dial-watching.	One (General Manager).
13. Investment banking. Member of group.	None.	One (Managing Director).
14. Development banking.	53; market and financial analyzing, clerical skills.	None.
15. Toy manufacturing.	250 (1,000 expectation); moderate skills–can be trained in 6 months to one year.	3 or 4.
16. Production of bulk vegetable oil.	7; machine operating.	None.
17. Manufacture of television antennas.	4; engineering, accounting.	One.
18. Refining of lubricating oil for Taiwan market.	226; dial-watching, trouble-shooting, engineering.	Two.
19. Manufacture and marketing of dairy products.	60; both high and low skills.	None.
20. Manufacture and marketing of consumer personal products.	250.	None.
21. Manufacture of electronic components.	650; moderate skills.	One.
22. Manufacture of electronic components and complete units.	1,200; high and moderate skills.	Four.
23. Manufacture of human pharmaceuticals, animal health and feed products.	210; high management and technical skills for manufacturing and marketing.	One.
24. Manufacture of pharmaceuticals.	At time of inquiry plant was not yet in operation; semi-skilled workers will be required.	None anticipated.

Employment and Job Skills

Since a prime objective of the program to attract foreign capital is to create jobs, a key factor in assessing the contribution of American corporations is how much indigenous employment has been created. A secondary point of interest is the extent to which local management talent is utilized, as evidenced by the number of Americans resident in Taiwan to oversee the operation. The pattern is shown in Table 10.

From this sample it is apparent that there is a wide variation in the number of jobs created by individual American companies. In aggregate, however, the factories established by private foreign capital have provided substantial employment in Taiwan. It is estimated that 150,000 additional jobs are needed each year to keep pace with the population growth rate and prevent unemployment from rising. In 1966, 723 new factories were established in Taiwan by foreign private corporations. These 723 new factories created 30,000 new job openings, or 20 percent of the annual job goal.[17]

The relatively large number of trained professional management and technical persons was a factor in attracting industry to Taiwan. One corporate Vice-President, whose capital-intensive Taiwan operation utilizes technically trained personnel, said, "In Taiwan trained people work at lower levels than anywhere else. There were many trained engineers among the refugees from the mainland who were working as porters." The net effect of this reservoir of local talent was that, to the mutual advantage of both the corporations and the Chinese government (who would naturally prefer to see their own nationals assume management as well as supervisory and labor positions), very few Americans were assigned as resident managers in Taiwan. This is indicated in Table 10.

The Chinese attitude was expressed by T. Y. Hsiung, Assistant Director of the Chinese Investment and Trade Office in New York City. Mr. Hsiung said,

> It is best to minimize the number of American residents. Usually the managers sent abroad for extended tours to any country are not the best. Then problems occur. It is best to send one or two top personnel who can run the whole operation. A Chinese assistant then will overcome the language problem.[18]

Transfer of Skills and Knowledge

Foreign investment not only provides employment but elevates the level of on-the-job competence and work sophistication through the provision of training. In addition to providing a variety of corporate training programs, foreign licensors are a source of knowledge and skill and indeed are fundamentally compensated with royalties for their technical know-how. The nature of the training veers from informal, on-the-job training, generally supervised, at least at first, by several Americans, to the formal schools that one company has in Tokyo and Manila for specialized training of sales engineers and repairmen.

The more common procedure is to train high-echelon Chinese supervisors in the pertinent factory or engineering operations at appropriate plants in the United States. These supervisors then return to Taiwan and train the next echelon, who in turn instruct the group below them, and so on. Often job functions of a specialized nature receive particular attention, either by arrangement for training in the United States or by sending appropriate specialists to Taiwan. Also, it is common for American supervisory and quality-control personnel to help start the factory operation. After some months, when it is deemed that the facility is properly "on-stream" and local personnel are able to assume responsibility, the Americans depart. For several companies, such personnel constitute factory start-up teams, which continually travel to new facilities throughout the world for this purpose.

One electronics company has an exchange program whereby, for a period of time, American foremen work in the Taiwan plant and Taiwanese foremen receive on-the-job training in American plants.

Licensor companies are commonly compensated specifically for imparting certain technical information through training in relevant technology.

Twenty-four of the 28 corporations that provided information with regard to training have programs as described.

Of the four companies that do not provide training, two were banks with minority interests. In one case, the bank participates in a going development bank operation in which training had already been provided. The other bank contended that the linguistic gap presented too many difficulties to train financial analysts. A parallel was drawn with an operation in the Philippines, where training was said to be easily accomplished because the English language was understood and knowledge of corporate finance was not only culturally acceptable but was taught in courses, particularly in the Jesuit schools. The two other companies that do not provide training are small and hire few personnel for their Taiwan operation.

Importance of Investment Incentives

Company executives were queried about the meaningfulness of the various investment incentives of the Republic of China. While some responses were confined to the needs of specific companies, most of the answers had general pertinence.

The incentives that were posed to the interviewees and mail respondents for comment were the following:

1. Five-year tax holiday.
2. Capital-gains tax exemption.
3. Low corporate tax (maximum rate is 18 percent).
4. Accelerated depreciation.
5. Capital repatriation in U.S. dollars (up to 15 percent per year).
6. Kaohsiung Export Processing Zone.
7. Statutory assurance that the government will not expropriate within 20 years after start of activity.
8. Other incentives that may have been negotiated.

Twenty-two companies with investments in Taiwan gave judgments as to the relative importance of specific incentives. Companies with only license arrangements did not respond, as the incentive program was inapplicable to their operations.

The pattern of attitudes expressed toward the incentives is shown in Table 11.

Five-Year Tax Holiday and Other Tax Incentives

Eleven companies, including four offshore-sourcing and six local-market operations, said that the tax holiday is a meaningful incentive. Only three companies said that the tax holiday was one of the least meaningful incentives.

Perhaps fundamental to assessment of tax incentives as an important device to attract investment is that return on

Table 11

Incentives for Investing in Taiwan

| | Number of times mentioned as meaningful to decision | | | |
Incentive	Offshore Sourcing	Local Marketing	Other	Total
1. Five-year tax holiday	4	6	1	11
2. Capital-gains tax exemption	1	1	–	2
3. Low corporate taxes	2	3	2	7
4. Accelerated depreciation	–	2	1	3
5. Capital repatriation in U.S. dollars	–	4	3	7
6. Kaohsiung Export Processing Zone	1	–	1	2
7. Statutory assurance that the government will not expropriate within 20 years after start of activity	–	1	–	1
8. Other incentives: Duty-free imports if initial paid-in capital is at least $2,250,000	4	1	–	5
Ability to re-patriate earnings	–	1	1	2
Reinvested earnings up to 25 percent to be exempt from Chinese tax	–	1	1	2
Protection against foreign competitor who does not recognize patent rights[a]	–	1	–	1
Retain reinvested earnings up to 10 percent of capital stock per year up to $2,500,000[b]	–	1	–	1

[a]This was a negotiated incentive aimed at exclusion from the Taiwan market of Italian pharmaceutical manufacturers, who do not recognize patent rights.

[b]This incentive is not set forth in the statutes. Although it could not be confirmed, it must be assumed that this item resulted from negotiation in which the company sought to gain permission to substitute retained earnings, with no formal limitation as to repatriability, for paid-in capital, which may not be repatriated in excess of 15 percent per year. The Chinese government, by limiting this privilege to 10 percent of capital stock per year, was able to regulate this action.

investment, which is a prime yardstick for investment decision-making, reflects any tax savings and increases in attractiveness as tax liability is reduced.

Another factor is that companies with far-flung international operations are faced with a myriad of foreign tax patterns. A common aim is to match low-tax areas with those, such as India, which have rather high tax-rate structures, so as to strike a balance and place international operations on a viable footing.

The tax holiday, several companies pointed out, reduces cash flow needs during the early stage of activity and lessens a possible need for additional capital or loans. On the other hand, a basic factor, mentioned by almost all respondents and only partly offset by the opportunity of the larger companies to counterbalance high taxes elsewhere, is that tax savings in Taiwan are negated because U.S. taxes will be correspondingly increased by the amount not paid to Taiwan. There is no net profit advantage.

Chinese partners do not, of course, incur U.S. taxation, and to them there is a very tangible tax savings through association with an American concern.

It was also pointed out that a tax holiday during the initial years of a business operation is relatively unimportant, as profits at this stage are low. Tax exemption during the early years of a business does not really provide financial assistance when needed.

One author points to tax exemption as

> an irrational or purely psychological inducement in the sense that it may be instrumental in encouraging the initiation of new business, but there may be little relationship between the effect of the inducement or the need for the assistance and the amount of subsidy actually received.[19]

While half of the reporting companies said that tax concession was meaningful, none said that without it they would not have invested in Taiwan.

It is perhaps significant that only one company made mention of the China Act tax benefits. While it should not be presumed that the respondents were unaware of the tax advantages of the Act, under which almost all were eligible, it quite probably reflects the slight importance attached to marginal tax savings as a factor in overseas investment decision-making. Indeed, Aharoni asserts, on the basis of his empirical research, that income tax exemption was considered to be a "very weak stimulant" in bringing about an overseas-investment decision.[20]

It may be conjectured that the offshore-sourcing companies, whose paramount concern is low-cost labor, would have come to Taiwan in the absence of a tax holiday. If this were established, perhaps only selected activities could be made eligible for tax exemption. This presumably would narrow the base of tax exemption without affecting the inflow of capital.

On balance, however, it may be said that the evidence indicates that tax exemption is considered to be important by offshore-sourcing as well as other companies. The decision-making process is highly complex, and it is not possible to set precise values on the individual considerations that led to the investment decision.

Moreover, tax-exemption schemes are currently being adopted by developing nations throughout the world. It would therefore be competitively disadvantageous to be without one. Compared to tax-incentive programs in many other countries, the five-year duration of the Taiwan tax exemption is moderate.

The five-year tax holiday is just one of several incentives that relate to tax benefit. The low corporate income tax-rate structure and the accelerated-depreciation incentives were mentioned by seven and three companies, respectively.

As in the case of tax exemption, the low (18 percent) maximum corporate rate was pointed to as providing an offset to the high tax rate incurred in other overseas areas.

The accelerated-depreciation feature, of course, reduces the amount of income for tax purposes during the early years but may result in an increased tax base during the later, postexemption years. It would appear that, notwithstanding some incidental U.S. tax benefits, depreciation deceleration would be more advantageous to the investor in the long run, when taxable income is higher. Both the low tax rate and accelerated-depreciation features must be regarded as long-term considerations, since during the initial five-year hiatus the features provide nonexistent benefits.

The incentive whereby reinvested earnings up to 25 percent of taxable income may be tax exempt (felt to be a meaningful feature by two companies) is likewise a futuristic concession.

While companies could theoretically divest, upon expiration of the tax holiday, at least 45 percent of their capital, and 15 percent per year thereafter, and could reinvest in another tax-exempt country, it would seem to be an unlikely, costly, and disruptive action. There is a question, therefore, whether tax concessions that are meaningful to investors only after cessation of the tax holiday are indeed consequential in the initial investment decision.

Neither the interviews nor the mail questionnaires elicited any evidence of long-term consideration of these features. Indeed, only one company made note of the China Act, which provides continuing tax benefit in the future.

While the accelerated-depreciation benefits would presumably have largely expired by cessation of the tax holiday,making loss of tax revenue to the Republic of China from this concession nominal, this would not be true of the low tax rates, which continue indefinitely.

Does this low corporate tax-rate structure merit review in this light? It would appear so. The tax exemption for reinvested earnings, on the other hand, tangibly contributes to increased investment of capital and is not subject to question on the same grounds.

While aspects of the tax-incentive program may be questioned, a quantitative cost-benefit calculation which would provide a tangible measure is not possible, as income data is unavailable and an answer to the question "What would have happened if (the tax exemption were for four years instead of five, etc.)?" is not possible. Therefore, the loss of tax revenue cannot be determined.

The Kaohsiung Export Processing Zone

The Government of the Republic of China formally dedicated the Kaohsiung Export Processing Zone(KEPZ) in December 1966. The KEPZ is a fenced and guarded industrial site on Kaohsiung Harbor, and was established to accommodate labor-intensive plants that manufacture, process, or assemble for export. In addition to the conventional free-trade-zone feature that goods may be imported and exported free of duty, the KEPZ offers the resource of Taiwan's low-cost skilled labor to facilitate manufacture, assurance of cheap power and water, and a choice of purchasing a standard factory building on a ten-year installment plan at a low rate or building a factory on leased land.

Naturally, the advantages of the KEPZ are pertinent only to labor-intensive, offshore-sourcing operations. Two of these companies expressed positive interest and believe the KEPZ to be a notable development. Indeed, one of the two was actively considering establishment of an operation in the Zone. The other company had established its operation several years before the KEPZ was constructed.

Although the KEPZ seems to be a success relative to its objectives (through March 1967 the KEPZ had already attracted half of the target number of plants, 61 percent of the invested capital goal, and almost 100 percent of the hoped-for 15,000 jobs had been created), the offshore-sourcing companies interviewed expressed many reservations. One electronics company questioned whether the close proximity of competing manufacturing operations might not lead to piracy of confidential technology and of skilled engineers. He also wondered whether the handful of American resident managers would be as happy as they would be in the Taipei area, which has schools for foreign children and other amenities. Several other companies, who had visited the Zone before it was operational, expressed skepticism over the accessibility of the area to both goods, which must be brought in by bonded truck, and workers.

There thus appeared to be no groundswell of enthusiasm for the KEPZ among the companies interviewed. It must be noted that the companies spoken to had conducted their investigations when KEPZ was a mere concept. Moreover it may be surmised that the shortcomings found in the KEPZ will be avoided if possible in the new free-trade zone that is being contemplated elsewhere in the Kaohsiung area.

It may be further noted that both the Republic of Korea and the Philippines were sufficiently impressed with the early results of the KEPZ to establish similar zones.

Repatriation of Capital

Eight companies indicated that the ability to repatriate capital was one of the most meaningful incentives offered to corporate investors by the Republic of China.

While none of the eight companies stated that they would repatriate capital, two companies avoided response to the question. The general reaction from most respondents was that the incentive feature was so important that if capital repatriation had not been assured, they probably would not have invested.

Offshore-sourcing companies did not regard the matter of capital repatriation as important. This may be attributable to the labor intensity of the operations and the relatively modest amount of capital invested.

One offical of a company with a high debt-to-equity ratio pointed out that the importance of the ability to repatriate capital was proportionate to the amount of equity involved. In his company's case, he believed, the feature was unimportant.

Only one company had a specific objection to the feature. The Vice-President of a bank said he believed the repatriation period, a shade under nine years, was too long.

Other Incentive Features

The exemption of capital gains from taxable income was noted as being meaningful by only two companies, both banks.

The general disinterest is primarily because there is little expectation of sale of assets. Spokesmen for two banks with Edge Act operations in Taiwan were concerned largely because of their role as financial advisor to American client corporations who might consider investment in Taiwan. They thought aspects of the treatment of capital gains were "cloudy."

The Statute for Encouragement of Investment clearly states that capital may be repatriated after two years at the rate of 15 percent a year and sets no restriction upon repatriation of profits. The Statute, however, does not specify the conditions for repatriation of capital gains either as to time limitation or as to whether such gain may be removed from Taiwan. One of the bank officials said that he had posed these questions some time ago, but clarification of such matters moves through the administration slowly.

Five companies, four of whom were offshore-sourcing operations, with paid-in capital in excess of $2,250,000, mentioned duty-free imports as being vital to their operation.

Three of these companies stated that they would not have invested in Taiwan if they had to pay duty upon imported components.

The statutory assurance by the Republic of China that assets will not be expropriated for at least twenty years evoked only one positive response. This interviewee, who had many years of international experience in developing nations, said that he considered it significant for a government to put an assurance such as this in writing. He pointed out that, while most countries who seek foreign investment offer some verbal warranty against expropriation, few countries commit themselves to a statutory guarantee.

Most company spokesmen offered the opinion that a guarantee against expropriation was meaningless, as the government might be overturned or the investment might change its form. The article in the Statute was viewed as a mere formality. One international division Vice-President said, "Expropriation in the future depends on the country's need for capital." Disbelief in the stabilty or the integrity of long-run commitments of foreign governments seems to be typical of American businessmen and has no specific reference to the Republic of China. Indeed, many interviewees cited recent expropriation incidents in Cuba, Indonesia, and other areas to explain their position. The attitude appears to stem not only from uncertainty as to the continuity and consistency of government but also from the imponderables of different cultures and standards.

Aharoni drew a similar conclusion from his study, particularly with regard to developing countries.

> When less developed countries were the subject of the discussion, it became clear that almost all respondents correlated 'less developed' with inefficient, nationalistic, unstable, and corrupt....The larger the discrepancy in habits, culture, and business conduct between a foreign country and the United States, the stronger the subjective uncertainty. [21]

The underlying attitudes illuminated by this reaction to the assurance against expropriation also serve to explain the general short-range outlook of most corporate investors, which has already been mentioned.

While the general reaction among interviewees was that the investment climate, the attitude of government officials, and the "incentive package" in Taiwan is excellent, three companies did not consider any of these factors to be particularly significant to their investment decision. One of these companies said that whatever contributes the most rapid return of capital was favored, without being specific. The tax concessions would probably be regarded as most favorable in this view. A second company, with a labor-intensive operation, said it "was overwhelmed with lower costs to the disregard of any incentives." A third company, which manufactures pharmaceuticals for sale in Taiwan, said that the size and potential of the Taiwan market overshadowed any incentives.

While these three companies were atypical in their expressed disregard of incentives, they manifested a hierarchy of priority held by many of the companies: subordination of incentive factors to those which serve to reduce risk and uncertainty. Fundamentally, it may be said that this desire to minimize risk and uncertainty is preeminent in importance among businessmen. To illustrate, the single most important reason why almost all the companies planning to serve the Taiwan market chose to invest in Taiwan was, as already cited, the negotiated concession or assurance that they would enjoy market protection in specific product categories if they would provide sufficient productive capacity to meet 100 percent of market needs. One company regarded as a major concession the negotiated agreement that competitive pharmaceutical imports from Italy, which does not recognize international drug patents, would be excluded. It is evident, in making an overview of corporate attitudes toward incentives—statutory or negotiated—that whatever will best assure profits and the safety of capital will supersede in importance factors that work toward maximization of gain. Thus, market protection and duty exemption for imports, which reduce the uncertainty of profits from local-market and offshore-sourcing activities, respectively, are more meaningful than tax concessions, which serve to increase profits only if profits are made. Just below, in order of importance, is the ability to minimize risk by pulling out if circumstances become adverse. Repatriability of capital is, therefore, a vital precondition to investment.

Perceived Political Risk in Taiwan

If the thesis set forth in the previous section is accepted—that is, factors that serve to minimize risk and uncertainty are more important in attracting overseas corporate investment than is the magnitude of profits or size of return on investment—then the perceived political climate of a country becomes all important to foreign investment.

In the case of natural-resources extraction, investment must seek the raw materials where they are to be found, and often a high degree of political risk must, perforce, be accepted, as with the oil industry in the Middle East. Taiwan, with negligible exploitable natural resources, was not a necessary risk for American corporate investors.

As a government that was defeated by the Communists on the mainland and in the process incurred the loss not only of the preponderant share of its homeland but the foreign investments located there, how was the Government of the Republic of China assessed by American corporate decision-makers? It was deemed best not to ask the question directly, as it was thought that respondents might feel compelled to filter out their own insights and emotionally based outlook and reply to a controversial political question with a prudent statement of company neutrality. And probably what is influential in corporate decision making is, not the apolitical stance that corporations take, but the deep-felt outlook toward the degree of political risk.

Furthermore, as one executive put it, "The AID investment insurance means that we don't have to consider political factors as much in our investment decisions." Despite the insurance, consideration of politically inspired change was voiced by every interviewee, knowledgeably or not. It must therefore be surmised that, while the assessment of political risk may not be a formal component of investment decision-making, it is nevertheless an integral, although less-articulated, factor, perhaps more greatly influenced by personal options than by more objective and formal criteria.

The question was posed late in the interviews, in the form of a request for a personal evaluation of the present and future political risks in Taiwan. Specific questions were asked about expectations of a flare-up of fighting, without specifying between whom; what might happen when Chiang Kai-shek died and whom his successor might be; and whether factional disputes and a government upheaval seemed to be a possibility.

Such open-end questions were impractical in a mail questionnaire. Instead, as may be noted in Exhibit III of the Appendix, Question 14 asked the respondents to rank six other countries with Taiwan in terms of greater, the same, or less political risk. The six countries listed for comparison represented a diversity of levels of political stability and economic development, and included past (Mexico and Brazil) as well as present expropriators (Algeria).

The varying backgrounds of respondents ranging from years of residence on and intimate knowledge of the mainland and Taiwan and friendships with Taiwanese and mainlander businessmen and government officials at all levels to quite limited understanding of the political background and situation of the island, reduces the meaningfulness of a precise quantitative tabulation of opinion.

Despite the differences in background, the tone of opinion among questionnaire respondents as well as among interviewees was generally similar. Almost every respondent foresaw continued stability with no major change expected. The general expectation among the spokesmen from the 27 companies that replied to the questions about political risk was for a continued stable and independent Taiwan, with the differences between mainlanders and Taiwanese gradually fading as cultural differences vanish. Three interviewees thought there might be some violence. Two of the three expect a conflict to erupt between Taiwanese and mainlanders when Chiang dies; a third executive thought it possible that Red China would blackmail Taiwan with the threat of dropping an atom bomb.

Overall a peaceful future for the island was foreseen. One corporate Vice-President, who had spent many years in Taiwan, thought that when Chiang died the ideology of return would be dropped and the separatism of the mainlander would lose its *raison d'être.* Prosperity was pointed to as a reason for continued stability. People increasingly have a vested interest in peace and economic growth.

There was expectation that Chiang's son Chiang Ching-kuo would replace him in a constitutionally ordered succession.

The questionnaire response echoed the interviewees' expectations of political stability and orderly change. While Great Britain and Japan were judged to be less politically risky than

Taiwan, as would be expected, Taiwan was judged to represent less risk to investment than the other four countries.

The tabulated comparison is shown in Table 12. Several executives who were interviewed had been associated with their company's ventures on the Chinese mainland before 1950 and were acquainted with their company's top-level management personnel in Taiwan and many Chinese government officials since those days.

An unspoken but clearly implied judgment, as these executives nostalgically recalled "the good old days" on the mainland, was that Taiwan, their remaining tie to the past, also represented a possible link to the future should conditions change. All of this is sheer speculation at this point of time. Nonetheless, the dimension of the mainland Chinese market, which has tantalized American businessmen since the late 19th century, still is alive in the minds of at least some older business executives.

Protective Devices

While the general expectation was for continued political stability, prudent businessmen, in order to minimize risk and uncertainty, took certain actions to protect invested capital.

The twenty companies interviewed were questioned as to their methods of reducing risk to their venture in Taiwan. Three of the companies had a licensing agreement which may be considered to be the safest form of overseas activity and is often undertaken as a first venture in order "to get one's feet wet" in a new market. Although eligible, none of these companies elected to obtain AID insurance. Of the 17 interviewed companies with equity investments in Taiwan, 16 had contracted with AID for the investment guaranties covering convertibility, expropriation, and war risk.

The spokesman for the one company which hadn't taken out this insurance said that his company is loathe to accede to the buy-American stipulation imposed by the U.S. government, because of the much higher costs that would be involved.

The use of local funds for equity or borrowing is another common means of reducing the possible loss from currency devaluation. In the event of expropriation, the lender would be left "holding part of the bag." Seven companies considered use of local funds in Taiwan in this light.

Table 12

Degree of Investment Risk
Compared with Other Countries

Country	Greater	Same	Less
Great Britain	6	1	—
Algeria	—	1	6
Japan	4	3	1
Brazil	—	1	8
Mexico	2	3	3
Liberia	—	2	5
	12	11	23

A high debt-to-equity ratio is an extension of the use of local borrowed funds to minimize risk, even if the funds are borrowed in the United States. Paid-in capital, which is more vulnerable because it must legally remain longer, may be reduced by the amount of borrowing.

An equity may be not only thin but small, and risk is thereby reduced in absolute terms.

Joining with a local partner is felt to be another means of minimizing the uncertainty and risk that a corporate outsider may experience.

For offshore-sourcing companies, a major concern, aside from anxiety over possible financial loss, is the loss of a key assembly link in a far-flung manufacturing operation, which could seriously disrupt the entire production process of items primarily intended for the U.S. market. One company, with this factor in mind, pointed out that they had an identical operation in Mexico, so that their risk was reduced.

The companies that produce for the Taiwan market are not faced with the massive production disruption that closure of the Taiwan facility entails for offshore-sourcing operations. Rather, they would merely lose the Taiwan market sales and profits. One interviewee, in pointing this out, emphasized the economic scale of the plant to fit the Taiwan market, which reflected a limited equity as well as limited market-loss risk.

The use of local subcontractors and the gradual substitution of more easily repatriable borrowed funds for equity over a period of time were other methods mentioned for reducing risk.

The future sale of stock in the local operation to Taiwanese, which in essence would give them local partners, was planned by two companies.

The tabulation of the interview response is set forth in Table 13.

Assessment of Results of Taiwan Operation

Company spokesmen and respondents were asked to evaluate the results of their Taiwan venture.

Answers to such a question are naturally highly subjective and not really meaningful in the absence of knowledge as to the

Table 13

Methods of Reducing Risk and Uncertainty

Means of reducing risk	Number of times mentioned by an interviewed company
AID Investment Guaranties	16
Local Funds Available (for equity and/or loans)	7
Joint Venture with Local Company	5
High Debt-to-Equity Ratio	5
Small Equity Investment	4
Licensing Arrangement	3
Future Stock Sale	2
Plant Just for Local Market	1
Repatriation of Capital by Substituting Borrowed Funds	1
Use of Subcontractors to Fabricate	1
Similar Operation in Mexico	1

"bullish" or "bearish" bias of the budget and the projections against which results are compared. Nevertheless, such a question can bring out acute divergencies from expectations, suggesting either a general or a specific problem. Conversely, on the positive side, above-favorable performance may suggest certain opportunities and advantages in Taiwan that were not previously evident.

A judgment was considered premature by seven companies, as their operations were not yet "on stream."

Nineteen companies commented upon operating results. Eleven companies stated that results were as expected, while the remaining eight companies split evenly between results found to be above and below expectations.

The reasons given for better-than-expected performance were the high rate of economic growth of Taiwan and the quality of the Chinese management and labor force. One company spokesman said, "The bulk of the Chinese labor force is literate, intelligent, industrious, and very trainable." Another interviewee, the Vice-President for international operations of his company, with worldwide responsibilities, attributes the better-than-expected success of his company's operation to "the Chinese cultural propensity as businessmen, traders, and practical people, further heightened because 'the best' survived the mainland."

On the negative side, one company pointed to subpar productivity as the reason for lower-than-projected operating results. The company stated this reason in a questionnaire and didn't elaborate. Two companies had lower sales than expected in the Taiwan market—one because of "tough competition," and the other because the anticipated demand for their product by a government agency failed to materialize.

One offshore-sourcing company, whose questionnaire was signed by the Quality Control Manager, stated in strong terms that results relative to forecast were not good because of raw material problems. It was not divulged what the subject materials were or what corrective measures might be possible. The seriousness of the problem was not quantified in terms of higher manufacturing costs, so that it is not possible to assess the magnitude of difficulty in this specific instance.

Other companies pointed out problems but indicated that they were not serious. Most of these problems centered upon relationships with lower-level civil servants, such as over-zealous customs inspectors and officials who levied nuisance taxes. The taxes were always successfully appealed in higher courts, and one interviewee judged that, as one moved up the bureaucratic ladder, a greater sense of fairness seemed to prevail.

Another executive pointed to nepotism and personal relationships as a cultural factor that made it difficult to fire an incompetent worker, since it might rebound unfavorably upon the sponsor who had facilitated the man's hire. He emphasized that although this problem had occurred, it was very rare and operating results were excellent.

Overall, the American companies surveyed were pleased with the performance of their activity.

Notes

1. The incentive features have been taken from the English-language texts of Republic of China, Industrial Development and Investment Center, *Statute for Investment by Foreign Nationals* (Taipei: February 1967); and Republic of China, Industrial Development and Investment Center, *Statute for Encouragement of Investment* (Taipei: November 1966).

2. For example, one that the writer attended was held on November 4, 1967, in New York, sponsored by the Chinese Institute of Engineers. Among the participants was the Director of the Investment Services Division, M. C. Liu, who came from Taipei for the occasion. Quite a few American corporate decision-makers were in the audience.

3. U.S., Embassy of the United States, Taipei, Taiwan, *Economic Trends of the Republic of China, Mid-year 1967* (Taipei, August 2, 1967), p. 5. (Mimeographed.)

4. *Statute for Investment by Foreign Nationals,* Article 3.

5. Unpublished data provided by CITO New York office, 1970.

6. Calculated from unpublished data provided by Mr. T. Y. Hsiung, Assistant Director, Chinese Investment and Trade Office, New York City, 1970.

7. Tillman Durdin, "Industrial Zone Helping Taiwan," New York *Times,* August 13, 1967, p. 13.

8. Liu, speech, November 4, 1967.

9. "America's 500 Largest Corporations," *Fortune,* June 15, 1967, pp. 194-228.

10. Raymond F. Mikesell, *U.S. Private and Government Investment Abroad* (Eugene, Oregon: University of Oregon Books, 1962), pp. 112-113.

11. Yair Aharoni, *The Foreign Investment Decision Process* (Boston: Division of Research, Graduate School of Business Administration, Harvard University, 1966), p. 95.

12. Raymond Vernon, "Multinational Enterprise and National Sovereignty," *Harvard Business Review,* March-April, 1967, pp. 156-172.

13. U.S. Department of Commerce, Office of Business Economics, *Survey of Current Business,* Vol. 7, No. 9, "International Investments of the United States in 1966," September 1967; and calculations therefrom.

14. Leo Model, "The Politics of Private Foreign Investment," *Foreign Affairs,* July 1967, pp. 639-651.

15. Liu, speech, November 4, 1967.

16. Aharoni, p. 98.

17. Republic of China, Chinese Investment and Trade Office, New York, "Industrial Investment Promotion Activities of the United States Office of the Chinese Investment and Trade Office, Republic of China," report submitted to United Nations Industrial Development Organization in June 1967 by T. Y. Hsiung, Assistant Director for First Meeting on Industrial Investment Promotion, New York, June 26-27, 1967.

18. Hsiung, speech on November 4, 1967, New York City, to Chinese Institute of Engineers and guests.

19. Milton C. Taylor, *Industrial Tax-Exemption in Puerto Rico* (Madison, Wisconsin: University of Wisconsin Press, 1957), p. 143.

20. Aharoni, p. 171.

21. Ibid., p. 94.

4   Summary and Implications

Based upon what American corporate investors say and do, to what extent do their motivations and expectations match the goals of the government of the Republic of China now and in the future?

Goals of the Republic of China

The Republic of China sees foreign private capital as a vehicle for providing jobs and evening the balance of payments during a developmental period of indeterminate length. The Chinese government does not see attraction of foreign capital as an interminable need.

The normal course of urbanization, coupled with a vigorous family planning program, ultimately should sufficiently lower the population growth rate to reduce the need to create new jobs.

Further economic growth will lean heavily upon industrialization, while the agricultural sector, with less growth potential because of limited arable land, will continue to diversify in response to profitable opportunity. Both sectors will produce largely for export, and at some future point attainment and maintenance of a favorable trade-and-payments balance should be a realizable goal.

It is during the current initial stage, when import of the means of production exceeds export of the results of production, that foreign capital and exchange is needed to cover the gap. To pursue the goals set forth, the Republic of China expects to continue certain domestic policies during this developmental period.

Labor rates must be continued at the present low level, both to remain competitive with other Asian countries and therefore attractive to foreign investors and to help generate investment capital from profitable domestic industry. The cost of living and inflation must continue to be restrained, so as to minimize pressure for wage increases and to preserve social and political, as well as economic, stability.

To carry out these programs, of necessity, means a continuance of denial of certain liberties for the people. For example, to help restrain wage increases and maintain stability, private labor unions would probably not be allowed to organize.

To the extent that the "brain drain" is caused by lack of monetary reward, rather than intellectual repression, government actions are moving in the direction of reducing the problem.

The political climate and thrust would therefore be to repress any movement which might threaten the status quo, while the economic thrust would be to vigorously accelerate industrial growth. Either internal strife between Taiwanese and mainlanders or an external flareup with the Communists would be anathema to the Nationalists' plans.

How long may this developmental period be expected to last before the Republic of China is able to be economically self-sufficient without the need for foreign funds?

A reduction in the annual rate of new job-seekers is not expected until at least 1986, and a significant decline probably not before 1991. This would be when 15-year-olds, born during the years when a sustained population growth rate decline started (1960) and a significant decline commenced (1966), would join the work force.

The current rate of industrialization is impressive, but Taiwan is still far below every nation in non-Communist Europe and Japan in absolute terms of gross national product per capita. To illustrate the current level of industrialization on a more basic level, an American executive pointed out that his company's plant in Taiwan was producing ultramodern electronic devices reflecting the most advanced technology but that even the workbenches had to be imported.

What this underscores is that, despite Taiwan's remarkable advances, continuing imports needed to foster industrialization will probably cause a trade deficit until completion of at least two more four-year plans (1976). This timing would obviously be affected by the vicissitudes of world sugar and other agricultural prices and of American spending in Vietnam.

We may anticipate, from this view of population growth and the need for imports to assist industrialization, that Taiwan's desire for foreign capital will continue until at least 1980. Whether the people will tolerate continuing restraints and whether the international situation will permit the necessary peaceful climate are imponderables which could far postpone the end of the developmental period and continue the need for foreign capital.

While the date may be questionable, the capabilities, recent achievements, and energies of the Chinese people insure the certainty of ultimate development.

Motivations and Expectations of American Corporate Investors

American corporations, it goes without saying, are fundamentally motivated to make profits. However, the magnitude of profit sought is tempered by a desire to minimize risk and uncertainty. Although the U.S. government has removed a large degree of the risk to invested capital through the AID investment guaranties, businessmen are inherently "gun-shy" and are interested in protecting their flow of earnings as well as equity.

Therefore, corporate executives frequently view their foreign investments from a short-range perspective, as long-range plans involve greater uncertainties. Within this perspective, funds are regarded as readily transferable, within legal limits, to more advantageous overseas or domestic investment situations regardless of national feelings.

Taiwan currently presents a situation to American businessmen of profitable opportunity and minimal risk. U.S. policy, as represented by the AID guaranty for investment in Taiwan and the potential protection from external threat afforded Taiwan by U.S. military forces, further reduces investment risk.

In addition to the present and foreseeable stability projected by the Chinese government and reinforced by the U.S. government, assured markets and tax concessions make profits more certain, but the almost instinctive desire to hasten the return of investment persists.

One may question whether the present confluence of interest of both the U.S. and Chinese governments vis-a-vis American private capital is likely to continue indefinitely. Any accommodation by the United States toward the Communists in Asia is likely to have a negative effect upon the Nationalists on Taiwan. For example, the recent softening of the U.S. attitude toward importation of goods from Communist China may have effect upon the way American businessmen will view Taiwan. The attractiveness of the mainland Chinese market is bound'to have substantial impact upon American businessmen, as it has traditionally and as it has upon German and other European and Japanese businessmen at this time. How trade opportunities on the mainland might affect American business perspective toward Taiwan is of course wholly conjectural, but it is a development certainly within the realm of possibility.

Domestic considerations in the United States are of more current importance to American business actions in Taiwan. The balance of payments situation and the U.S. commitment in Vietnam (to the relative neglect of domestic urban needs) may increase pressure to keep dollars from going abroad, even to friendly developing countries. Instead, the consideration that dollars invested domestically could create needed jobs for the poor could become a factor in American politics.

The political leverage of Taiwan with the United States is directly proportionate to the "heat" of events in Vietnam or North Korean pressures. The Nationalist armed forces are a strategic reserve that ties up Chinese Communist troops in Fukien and, consequently, keeps them away from the Vietnam border. Chinese Nationalist forces, therefore, serve a meaningful purpose, consonant with U.S. aims at this time. Were the war to end, however, this importance would decline. Indeed, Chiang's petulance and expression of the "ideology of counterattack" is a continuous source of embarrassment that the United States repeatedly tries to underplay.

On balance, then, it may be questioned whether future U.S. political and economic interests will continue to be as favorable toward Taiwan and, therefore, toward private American investment in Taiwan. Should mutual interests coincide to a lesser degree, American corporate antennae may perceive the degree of business risk in Taiwan in a less positive way.

Even at this time, protective devices which include borrowed funds (local or American), joint ventures, high debt-to-equity ratios, and substitution of repatriable earnings for investment capital are used by almost all American corporations in Taiwan. These actions underscore the importance of minimization of risk to businessmen.

Compatibility of Goals

The developmental period tactics of the Chinese government—to maintain the present low wage pattern, guard against inflation, and strive to preserve economic as well as political and social stability—closely match the investment criteria of American businessmen. Low wages and a steady level of material costs contribute to profits, and general stability reduces uncertainty. Equally important is the positive attitude projected toward private foreign businessmen—particularly by Chinese economic officials, who genuinely want foreign investment. And businessmen are not adverse to being courted, especially in the context of profit-making.

While bureaucratic red tape and cultural differences, which are manifested by a greater amount of negotiation and fluidity of arrangement than takes place in the United States, are a source of complaint by many American businessmen, the frank acknowledgement of the problem by the Chinese industrial-development leaders and their sometimes successful efforts to provide relief tend largely to off-set the inconveniences. The Chinese industrial-development program has been especially fortunate to have men who are able to understand and to communicate to American business leaders in their own frame of reference.

Taiwan's incentive program is competitive with those of other developing countries but not so generous as to deprive the nation of needed tax revenue, although the 18 percent maximum tax rate might be questioned as being too low. The tax rate might perhaps be restructured to reward foreign investors for the number of jobs they directly or indirectly create, training provided, and/or net export sales they generate. Suitable tax deductions might motivate established foreign investors toward these economically and socially desirable goals. It is unlikely that a moderately higher tax-rate structure would discourage investors.

In the long term, when the Taiwan economy is sustainable without the need for foreign investment, a different attitude on the part of the Chinese government should be expected. At that time, Taiwanese will probably air the universal complaints of host-country nationals: that research and development is all imported and local activity in certain industries is discouraged; that top management positions are generally unavailable to them; that the local operation is subject to manipulation for worldwide corporate reasons; and that the preponderant resources of American corporate capital and technology restrict local development in peripheral fields.

More important, at that future date foreign-owned activities will be extracting a flow of earnings from the Taiwan economy, and their contribution will be questioned. Superimposed upon a pent-up demand for higher wages and a political atmosphere in which there is little outlet for frustrations, foreign-owned enterprise might easily become a scapegoat.

The Chinese government at such a time would no longer encourage foreign investment, and the possibility of expropriation would be very real. Should the U.S. government continue its present policies and legal framework through the end of the developmental period in Taiwan (the AID investment guarantees, and the China Trade Act), certain inconsistencies would exist. The stimulants to overseas investment would no longer serve the valid purpose that they do now. The need to protect its investment guarantees might involve the United States in internal matters, much to its political disadvantage and against its ideals. That the AID investment guarantees have long-term political implications that may not reflect changed circumstances is something that should be considered at this time.

It may be that offshore-sourcing operations are an exception to this possible long-term divergence of interest. Perhaps. But in a future of large supersonic air transports and greater spread in labor costs between the United States and Taiwan, the temptation to expand the scope and number of offshore-sourcing activities will surely arouse reaction in the United States, particularly among labor unions and supplier companies.

Overall, while in the short term the goals of American corporate investors and those of the Chinese government are in harmony, in the longer term, as Chinese developmental aims are realized, a dissonance is to be expected.

Perhaps the wisest course for American companies is to emulate one corporation and plan to sell shares of stock to the Chinese public (including employees) as soon as the operation is suitably established. While this would be no panacea, it should help to moderate future tensions.

From this study of the involvement of American private capital in Taiwan, there appears to be little that is transferable to other developing countries as object lessons for their own development. The Chinese cultural traditions of hard work and saving; the escape from the mainland of some of the most highly trained persons; the legacy of literacy and infrastructure, particularly agricultural, left by the Japanese; and the propitious timing of the Korean War with resultant massive United States aid that provided further infrastructure were the major ingredients of rapid Chinese economic growth. Private foreign capital helped development but, unless the preceding conditions had existed, would have achieved little by itself. It has served a largely catalytic effect, replacing the similar role served by government aid.

Perhaps the best lesson that Taiwan might provide to other developing nations is a tangible example of successful development, which might reverse the self-defeating sense of futility so evident in many areas of the world. Maybe the example of the payoff of hard work and goal-directedness can engender constructive attitudes and actions.

Overall, the most important ingredient for successful development would appear to be not only enlightened leadership and capital but an industrious and energetic population. This last attribute certainly characterizes the Chinese on Taiwan.

Appendix

Methodology

METHODOLOGY

The data and information with regard to actions, attitudes, and intentions of American corporations and corporate executives was obtained from personal interviews and from questionnaires.

Personal Interviews

Lists of United States corporations with direct investment or licensing activity in Taiwan were obtained from the Chinese Investment and Trade Office in New York. Letters were then sent to a sample representing a substantial number of these companies (24 of 61 firms listed as having investment or technical assistance activity in Taiwan). The companies were selected judgmentally, with the criteria of bigness and with the aim of getting a representation of different industries. Standard corporate data sources, such as *Standard and Poors,* were used to evaluate the companies.

Letters were generally addressed to corporate presidents and included a list of general questions with regard to the Taiwan activity. (See Exhibit 1.)

Twenty of the 24 companies granted interviews. Two companies, it turned out, had applied for permission to invest in Taiwan but had not yet made a decision to do so and declined to discuss the matter at that time. Two other companies refused to grant interviews because of their policy toward disclosure of "such confidential business matters."

Interviews lasted from 1 hour and 15 minutes to almost 3 hours in one case. Most were slightly over 2 hours.

The actual interviews were conducted with one or two executives who directed the Taiwan activity and/or were involved in the investment decision. Often the interviewees would call in other persons in their company or obtain relevant files to answer specific questions. The confidentiality of the interviews was stressed prior to and at the conclusion of the talks. The interviews themselves included the general questions noted on the initial list but ranged far beyond. The purpose of the sample questions was to give company presidents, to whom most of the letters were addressed, a chance to see the thrust of the investigation, with the hope that they would then assent to an interview with the appropriate executive or executives. The thought was that this approach would eliminate any anxiety the interviewees might have had about answering certain questions for fear of transgressing company security policy.

The list of questions also alerted interviewed executives to the need to get pertinent files and to insure the availability of involved staff experts. This saved considerable time and enhanced interview efficiency and yield.

The interviews were conducted in a nondirective manner unless the interviewee veered toward digression from the subject of Taiwan and company overseas-investment policies. A broad outline of questions, including those initially sent to the companies, was used to guide the interview. (See Exhibit 2.)

Sometimes specific information was unavailable at the time of the interview or questions arose during the review of interview notes. Follow-up telephone calls elicited subsequent information.

Interviewees were invariably cooperative and generally enthusiastic about the subject area of corporate investment policies and procedures.

Questionnaire

A five-page questionnaire (Exhibit 3) was sent to twenty-four companies with activity in Taiwan other than those from whom interviews were requested. Ten completed and two partially completed questionnaires were returned. Eight companies declined to fill in the questionnaire, either because they hadn't made a decision regarding a Taiwan project or because they didn't want to disclose information or take the time to fill out a lengthy questionnaire.

Exhibit 1 General Questions with Regard to Taiwan Investment

General Questions with Regard to Taiwan Investment

1. Corporate criteria and policies for overseas investments.

2. Relative importance to an investment decision of
   (a) payout period?
   (b) size of investment?
   (c) control?
   (d) size of market?
   (e) competition?
   (f) maintenance of market position?
   (g) availability of local capital?
   (h) other considerations?

3. Decision process:
   (a) How and when initial consideration of Taiwan project was initiated?
   (b) Progression of project—What was the nature of the investigation? Who was involved? How long did it take?
   (c) Decision—What and when?
   (d) What echelons were involved at each stage of the process?

4. What were the key factors that led to your decision to invest in Taiwan?

5. Were there alternate investment opportunities considered but rejected in favor of the Taiwan venture? If so, why were they rejected?

6. How would you rate, in order of importance, the following concessions to invest offered by the Taiwan government:
   (a) Five-year income tax holiday?
   (b) Corporate income tax-rate ceiling of 18 percent?
   (c) Exemption from taxation of reinvested earnings up to 25 percent of taxable income?
   (d) Capital-gains exemption from income tax?
   (e) Tax-deductible reserve (up to 7 percent) to help safeguard against foreign exchange loss?
   (f) Kaohsiung Export Processing Zone?

      (g) Accelerated depreciation?

      (h) Capital repatriation allowability (up to 15 percent per annum commencing two years after project completion)?

      (i) Agreement not to expropriate within twenty years after the start of business?

7. Have governmental authorities been cooperative throughout the investment procedure?

8. Is there any way in which American corporate investors might be better assisted by either Republic of China or American governmental authorities?

9. How do you evaluate the political risk in this venture?

10. How have the results to date measured up to expectation?

Exhibit 2   Question Guide for Interviewing

Question Guide for Interviewing

1. General corporate criteria for overseas investments:
   - (a) Payout period?
   - (b) Size of investment?
   - (c) Size of market?
   - (d) Specific product categories?
   - (e) Competition?
   - (f) Preservation of market?
   - (g) Availability of local capital?
   - (h) Other (What)?

2. Decision process:
   - (a) How and when initial consideration of the Taiwan project was initiated?

     What was the importance of

     - (1) friend's recommendation?
     - (2) other company experience?
     - (3) U.S. Government?
     - (4) vulnerability to competition of export market?
     - (5) a deliberate search?
     - (6) solicitation by Taiwan government?
     - (7) other factors?

   - (b) Progression of project:

     What was the nature of the investigation?

     Who was involved?

     How much time was spent?

     What outside sources of information were utilized?

     What, if any, outside information was not used?

   - (c) What decision was made, and when?

     How did it compare to the initial proposal?

     Were there any negotiated concessions?

113

(d) What management echelons were involved at each stage of the investment decision process?

Were outside consultants used?

(e) How does the Taiwan investment compare to company investment in similar facilities in the United States and overseas in terms of
(1) scale - capacity of production facility
         capital requirements?

(2) debt-to-equity ratio?

(f) What was the form of capital:
   (1) U.S. dollars?   (4) Machinery (old)?
   (2) Local funds?   (5) Raw material and parts?
   (3) Machinery (new)?   (6) Technical know-how?

3. What were the key factors that led to decision to invest in Taiwan:

   (a) Cheap labor?
   (b) Readily trainable labor?
   (c) Political stability?
   (d) Little "red tape"?
   (e) Nice place for American management to live?
   (f) Availability of U.S. dollars for repatriation?
   (g) Minimal government interference?
   (h) Geographic situation?
   (i) Availability of water and power?
   (j) Other factors?

4. Were there alternate investment opportunities considered but rejected in favor of the Taiwan venture? If so, what were they?

5. How important to the investment decision were incentives offered by the Taiwan government (rank in order of importance):

Exhibit 2 115

(a) Five-year tax holiday?

(b) Eighteen percent maximum corporate income tax rate?

(c) Tax exemption for reinvested earnings up to 25 percent of taxable income?

(d) Capital-gains exemption from income tax?

(e) Seven percent tax-deductible reserve permitted to protect against foreign-exchange loss on debts in connection with purchase of productive equipment?

(f) Accelerated depreciation?

(g) Kaohsiung Export Processing Zone?

(h) Capital repatriation (15 percent per year—two years after project completion)?

(i) The Chinese government's insurance that it will not expropriate within twenty years after commencement of the business?

(j) Other incentives?

Why were _____ most important? Why were _____ not important?

What additional concessions would you want?

Would you have rejected the investment if any of the above were not offered?

6. Have you found governmental authorities to be helpful? How?

U.S. governmental agencies? Republic of China agencies?

7. Are there areas of improvement that you can suggest in the way governmental agencies serve business investment needs?

8. How do you evaluate the present and future political risk in Taiwan (re: flare-up of fighting; death of Chiang Kai-shek and uncertainty as to his successor; government upheaval and factional disputes)?

Are there any ways you have tried to reduce the risk in the Taiwan venture?

How do you feel about joining with local partners?

9. Have results lived up to expectation in your Taiwan venture:

   (a) Sales results?
   (b) Manufacturing costs—labor, raw materials, transportation?
   (c) Other?

10. If the same opportunity were presented to you now, would you recommend an investment in Taiwan on the same basis?

    If not, what would you do differently, and why?

Exhibit 3　Questionnaire

QUESTIONNAIRE

Please answer all questions as applicable.

1. Does your company have any business interest in Taiwan (Formosa)?

    Yes....... No.......

2. What is the nature of the activity? (Please check appropriate boxes)

    manufacturing and/or assembling ....
    sales office ....
    distributorship ....
    licensing arrangement ....
    mining/extraction ....
    other (please explain) ....

3. (a) Does the business activity indicated above involve an equity investment?

    Yes....... No.......

    (b) If "yes," how much is the:

    Total Investment ....
    Equity ....
    Debt Financing ....

4. (a) How did the initial debt to equity relationship compare to that of other of your company's overseas ventures?

    about the same ....
    greater debt ....
    greater equity ....

(b) How did the debt to equity relationship compare to that of your company's domestic (U.S.) ventures?

about the same   ....
greater debt   ....
greater equity   ....

5. How many persons are employed? ....

6. How many of the employees are resident Americans? ....

7. How would you describe the nature of the work, and the degree of skill and training required for most of the employees?

....
....
....

8. (a) Does your company provide the necessary training?

Yes....... No.......

(b) If "yes," what is the nature of the training?

....
....
....

9. (a) Is your company satisfied with:

availability of trainable labor   ....
productivity of labor   ....
physical facilities   ....
services   ....
ease of doing business in Taiwan   ....
other factors   ....

Exhibit 3   121

(b) Is your company dissatisfied with any of the above considerations?

Yes....... No.......

(c) If there is any dissatisfaction, what is it, and what would you attribute it to?

....
....
....

10. Has your company located its operation in Taiwan (Formosa) in order to serve:

the Taiwan market only   ....

Taiwan and other Asian markets   ....

as an "offshore source" for U.S.   ....

other markets (what?)   ....

11. What are the two or three most important reasons for your company's decision to invest in Taiwan rather than another overseas location?

(1) ....

(2) ....

(3) ....

(4) ....

12. What is your company doing, or planning to do, with earnings from the Taiwan venture during the first five years of operation?

repatriate to U.S. as dividends   ....

reinvest in Taiwan   ....

reinvest elsewhere   ....

13. (a) Of the following incentives to invest offered by the Republic of China Government for investment in Taiwan, indicate in the appropriate column the two that are most meaningful and the two that are least meaningful:

Incentive	Most Meaningful	Least Meaningful
(1) Five year tax holiday	....	....
(2) Capital gains income tax exemption	....	....
(3) "Low Corporate Taxes" (Maximum rate is 18%)	....	....
(4) Accelerated depreciation	....	....
(5) Capital repatriation in U.S. $'s (15% per year is allowed, two years after project completion)	....	....
(6) Kaohsiung Export Processing Zone	....	....
(7) Statutory assurance that the government will not expropriate within twenty years after commencement of the venture	....	....
(8) Other incentives (please explain)	....	....

(b) Why were the checked incentives most meaningful to your company?

....
....
....
....

Exhibit 3   123

(c) Why were the checked incentives least meaningful to your company?

....
....
....
....

14. Considering world conditions and the political and economic climate on Taiwan, how do you regard the degree of risk inherent in your venture? Please check under the appropriate column next to each country to indicate how you assess the amount of risk in Taiwan would compare to a similar investment in that country:

Country	Degree of Risk in Taiwan		
	Greater	Same	Less
Great Britain	....	....	....
Algeria	....	....	....
Japan	....	....	....
Brazil	....	....	....
Mexico	....	....	....
Liberia	....	....	....

15. (a) Have results lived up to expectations in your Company's Taiwan venture? Please check under appropriate column for items that are applicable:

	Results Relative to Forecast are		
	Better	Same as	Not as good
Sales (Taiwan Market)	....	....	....
Manufacturing Costs	....	....	....
Labor	....	....	....
Raw Materials	....	....	....
Transportation	....	....	....
Worker Productivity	....	....	....

(b) How do you account for those results indicated above that have been better than forecast?

....

....

....

(c) How do you account for those results indicated above that are not as good as forecast?

....

....

....

Thank you very much for taking the time to answer this questionnaire. All information that you supplied will be treated with confidence. Neither your name nor your company name will be divulged. Please indicate if you would like a copy of the completed report.

Bibliography

BIBLIOGRAPHY

This bibliography is divided into three categories: books and journals, public documents and statements, and magazine and newspaper articles. Unless otherwise indicated, the references are in English.

Books and Journals

Aharoni, Yair. *The Foreign Investment Decision Process.* Boston: Harvard University, Graduate School of Business Administration, Division of Research, 1966.

Ballantine, Joseph. *Formosa.* Washington, D.C.: The Brookings Institution, 1952.

Barclay, George W. *Colonial Development and Population in Taiwan.* Princeton, New Jersey: Princeton University Press, 1954.

Barnett, Doak A. *Communist China and Asia.* New York: Vintage Books, Division of Random House by Arrangement with Council on Foreign Relations, 1961.

Carnegie Endowment for International Peace. Division of International Law. "The Sino-Japanese Negotiations of 1915." Pamphlet 45, 1921.

Cheng, Chen. *Land Reform in Taiwan.* Taipei: China Publishing Co., 1961.

Chiang Kai-shek. *China's Destiny.* Translated by Wang Chung-hui. New York: MacMillan, 1947.

Dennett, Tyler. *Americans in Eastern Asia.* New York: MacMillan, 1922.

Emery, Robert F. "Taiwan's Mushroom Industry: A Study in Export Growth." Report internally circulated at the Board of Governors of the Federal Reserve System, Division of International Finance, February 2, 1965.

Eto, Shinkichi. "An Outline of Formosan History." *Formosa Today.* Edited by Mark Mancall. New York: Praeger, 1964, 43-58.

Fairbank, John King. *The United States and China.* Rev. ed. New York: Viking Press (by arrangement with Harvard University Press), 1962.

Goddard, W. G. *Formosa: A Study in Chinese History.* East Lansing, Michigan: Michigan State University Press, 1966.

127

Gurtov, Melvin. "Recent Developments on Formosa." *China Quarterly,* 31 (July-September 1967), 59-95.

Harrison, Bryan. *Southeast Asia.* London: MacMillan, 1963.

House, Edward H. *The Japanese Expedition to Formosa.* Tokyo: 1875.

Hou Chi-ming. *Foreign Investment and Economic Development in China 1840-1937.* Cambridge, Mass.: Harvard University Press, 1965.

Hsieh Chiao-min. *Taiwan-Ilha Formosa.* Washington, D.C.: Butterworths, 1964.

Israel, John. "Politics on Formosa." *Formosa Today.* Edited by Mark Mancall. New York: Praeger, 1964, 59-67.

Jacoby, Neil H. *U.S. Aid to Taiwan.* New York: Praeger, 1966.

Joktik, Ong. "A Formosan's View of the Formosan Independence Movement." *Formosa Today.* Edited by Mark Mancall. New York: Praeger, 1964, 163-170.

Kallgren, Joyce. "Nationalist China's Armed Forces." *Formosa Today.* Edited by Mark Mancall. New York: Praeger, 1964, 91-100.

Kao, Charles Hsi-chung. "An Analysis of Agricultural Output Increase on Taiwan." *Journal of Asian Studies,* Vol. XXVI, No. 4 (August 1967), 611-626.

Kerr, George H. *Formosa Betrayed.* Boston: Houghton Mifflin Co., 1965.

Koen, Ross Y. *The China Lobby in American Politics.* New York: MacMillan, 1960.

Krause, Lawrence B., and Dam, Kenneth W. *Foreign Tax Treatment of Foreign Income.* Washington, D.C.: Brookings Institution, 1964.

Lockwood, William W. *The Economic Development of Japan.* Princeton, New Jersey: Princeton University Press, 1954.

Mancall, Mark. "Introduction." *Formosa Today.* Edited by Mark Mancall. New York: Praeger, 1964, 1-42.

Mei Wen-li. "The Intellectuals on Formosa." *Formosa Today.* Edited by Mark Mancall. New York: Praeger, 1964, 121-130.

Meisner, Maurice. "The Development of Formosan Nationalism." *Formosa Today.* Edited by Mark Mancall. New York: Praeger, 1964, 147-162.

Mikesell, Raymond F. (ed.). *United States Private and Government Investment Abroad.* Eugene, Oregon: University of Oregon, 1962.

Model, Leo. "The Politics of Private Foreign Investment." *Foreign Affairs,* Vol. 45, No. 4 (July 1967), 639-651.

Riggs, Fred W. *Formosa Under Chinese Nationalist Rule.* New York: MacMillan, 1952.

Sun Yat-sen. *San Min Chu I* (translated by Frank W. Price). Shanghai: China Committee, Institute of Pacific Relations, 1927.

Taylor, Milton C. *Industrial Tax-Exemption in Puerto Rico.* Madison, Wisconsin: University of Wisconsin, 1957.

Van der Kroef, Justus M. "Philippine Communism and the Chinese." *China Quarterly,* 30 (April-June 1967), 115-148.

Vernon, Raymond. "Multinational Enterprise and National Sovereignty." *Harvard Business Review,* Vol. 45, No. 2 (March-April 1967), 156-172.

Whitman, Marina Von Neumann. *Government Risk-Sharing in Foreign Investment.* Princeton, New Jersey: Princeton University, 1965.

Yang, J. Y. "The Tea of China and Formosa." *Far East Economic Review,* XIV (October 2, 1952).

Yen, Sophia Su-fei. *Taiwan in China's Foreign Relations: 1836-1964.* Hamden, Connecticut: Shoe String Press, Inc., 1965.

Public Documents and Statements

Republic of China

Hsiung, T. Y. "Investment Climate in Taiwan." Statements made at seminar on Industrial Opportunities in Taiwan, sponsored by Chinese Institute of Engineers, New York, N. Y., November 4, 1967.

Liu, M. C. "Investment Opportunities in Taiwan, Republic of China." Speech presented at seminar on Industrial Opportunities in Taiwan, sponsored by Chinese Institute of Engineers, New York, N. Y., November 4, 1967.

Republic of China. Chinese Investment and Trade Office. *Industrial Investment Promotion Activities.* Unpublished report submitted to United Nations Industrial Development Organization, June 1967.

Republic of China. Council for International Economic Cooperation and Development. *A Brief Report on the Supply of Labor in Taiwan.* Taiwan: Industrial Development and Investment Center, June 1967 (in English).

Republic of China. Council for International Economic Cooperation and Development. *The Republic of China's Fourth Four-Year Plan for Economic Development of the Province of Taiwan: 1965-1968* (in English). Taiwan: November 1965.

Republic of China. Council for International Economic Cooperation and Development. *Statute for Encouragement of Investment.* Promulgated—September 10, 1960. Amended—January 4, 1965. English translation. Taiwan: Industrial Development and Investment Center, November 1966.

Republic of China. Council for International Economic Cooperation and Development. *Statute for Investment by Foreign Nationals.* Promulgated—July 14, 1954. Amended—December 14, 1959. English translation. Taiwan: Industrial Development and Investment Center, February 1967.

Republic of China. Council for International Economic Cooperation and Development. *Taiwan Statistical Data Book: 1966.* Taiwan: June 1966 (in English).

Republic of China. Taiwan Governor-General's Office. *Fifty-one Years of Statistical Abstracts of Taiwan.* Taipei: 1946 (in Chinese).

United Nations

United Nations. Economic Commission for Asia and the Far East. *Economic Survey of Asia and the Far East: 1966* (67. II. F. 1), Bangkok, 1967.

United States

U.S. AID Representative. *Fifteen Years of U.S. Economic Assistance to the Republic of China.* Taipei, Office of the U.S. AID Representative, September 1966.

U.S. Congress. Senate. Committee on Armed Services and Committee on Foreign Relations. *Military Situation in the Far East, Hearings* before the combined committees. 82d Cong., 1st sess., 1951.

U.S. Department of the Army, Office of the Chief of Military History. *United States Army in World War II, The War in the Pacific,* Vol. 4, "The Fall of the Philippines," Washington, D.C., 1953.

U.S. Department of Commerce. Bureau of International Commerce. *Principal Features of the China Trade Act.* Washington, D.C. December 15, 1965. (Mimeographed.)

U.S. Department of Commerce. Bureau of International Commerce. "World Trade Outlook," *International Commerce,* Vol. 73, No. 29, July 17, 1967, 43.

U.S. Department of Commerce. Bureau of International Commerce. "United States Overseas Promotions," *International Commerce,* Vol. 73, No. 32, August 7, 1967, 30.

U.S. Department of Commerce. Office of Business Economics. *Survey of Current Business,* Vol. 47, No. 9. "International Investments of the United States in 1966," September 1967.

U.S. Economic Cooperation Administration. Mission to China. *U.S. Economic Assistance to Formosa, 1 January to 31 December 1950.* Washington: Government Printing Office, 1951.

U.S. Embassy of the United States. Taipei, Taiwan, Republic of China. *The Taiwan Economy: 1958-66 Basic Data.* Taipei: American Embassy, October 1967.

U.S. Embassy of the United States. Taipei, Taiwan, Republic of China. *Economic Trends of the Republic of China.* Taipei: American Embassy, February 13, 1967. (Mimeographed.)

U.S. Embassy of the United States. Taipei, Taiwan, Republic of China. *Economic Trends of the Republic of China, Mid-year 1967.* Taipei: American Embassy, August 2, 1967. (Mimeographed.)

U.S. Internal Revenue Code of 1954. Section 941.

U.S. Internal Revenue Code of 1954. Section 943.

U.S. International Cooperation Administration. *Investment Guaranty Handbook.* Washington, D.C.: Government Printing Office, n.d.

U.S. Office of Naval Operations. *Taiwan (Formosa).* OPNAV 50E-12. Washington, D.C.: Office of the Chief of Naval Operations, Navy Department, 1944.

U.S. Office of Naval Operations. *Taiwan (Formosa): Economic Supplement.* OPNAV 50E-13. Washington, D.C.: Office of the Chief of Naval Operations, Navy Department, 1944.

U.S. Office of Naval Operations. *Taiwan (Formosa), the Pescadore Islands.* OPNAV 13-21. Washington, D.C.: Office of the Chief of Naval Operations, Navy Department, 1944.

U.S. Department of State. Division of Publications. Office of Public Affairs. *United States Relations with China with Special Reference to the Period 1944-1949.* Publication 3573. Far Eastern Series 30. Washington, D.C.: Government Printing Office, 1949.

U.S. Department of State. Division of Publications. Office of Public Affairs. "U.S. Policy Toward Formosa." *Bulletin,* January 16, 1950. 79-81.

U.S. Department of State. Division of Publications. Office of Public Affairs. "North Korean Forces Invade South Korea." *Bulletin,* July 3, 1950. 3-7.

U.S. Department of State. Division of Publications. Office of Public Affairs. "The Challenge of the Developing Countries," by David E. Bell. *Bulletin,* July 26, 1965. 173-177.

U.S. Strategic Bombing Survey. Over-all Economic Effects Division. *The Effects of Strategic Bombing on Japan's War Economy.* Washington, D.C.: Government Printing Office, December 1946.

Newspapers and Magazines

"America's 500 Largest Corporations," *Fortune Magazine,* July 15, 1967, 194-228.

Andrews, Frederick. "Taiwan: Healthy Upstart Attracts Capital," *New York Times,* January 20, 1967, 53.

De Onis, Juan. "Shortage of Resources Termed Major Deterrent to Birth Control," *New York Times,* April 15, 1967, 10.

Durdin, Tillman. "G.I.'s Find Taipei Nice Spot to Visit," *New York Times,* August 10, 1967, 10.

Feinstein, Selwyn. "Publishers on Taiwan Increase Their Sales of 'Pirated' Books," *Wall Street Journal,* May 29, 1967, 1.

"Formosan Independence Movement Appeal," *New York Times,* November 20, 1966, 20.

"IBRD [International Bank for Reconstruction and Development] Lends $15 million to China Development Corporation for Industrial Expansion and Modernization," *New York Times,* August 13, 1967, sec. 3, 34.

"Restrictions announced on American private overseas investments," *Wall Street Journal,* January 3, 1968, 1.

About the Author

Jordan C. Schreiber is a Senior Security Analyst with Shields and Company in New York City and a part-time member of the faculty of New York University. A graduate of the University of Oklahoma, he received his M.B.A. from the Harvard Business School and his Ph.D. from New York University.